CENTER
CENTER

CENTER
CENTER

A FUNNY, SEXY, SAD

ALMOST-MEMOIR

OF A BOY IN BALLET

JAMES WHITESIDE

VIKING

VIKING
An imprint of Penguin Random House LLC
penguinrandomhouse.com

Illustrations by Teddy O'Connor

LIBRARY OF CONGRESS CATALOGING-IN-PUBLICATION DATA
Names: Whiteside, James, author.
Title: Center center : a funny, sexy, sad almost-memoir of a boy in ballet / James Whiteside.
Description: New York : Viking, [2021] |
Identifiers: LCCN 2021001323 (print) | LCCN 2021001324 (ebook) |
ISBN 9780593297834 (hardcover) | ISBN 9780593297841 (ebook)
Subjects: LCSH: Ballet dancers—United States—Biography. | American Ballet Theatre. |
Male dancers—United States—Biography. | Sexual minorities—United States—Biography.
Classification: LCC GV1785.W445 A3 2021 (print) | LCC GV1785.W445 (ebook) |
DDC 792.802/8092 [B]—dc23
LC record available at https://lccn.loc.gov/2021001323
·LC ebook record available at https://lccn.loc.gov/2021001324

Printed in the United States of America
1st Printing

BOOK DESIGN BY LUCIA BERNARD

Many names and identifying characteristics have been changed
to protect the privacy of the individuals involved.

For my mother, Nancy

CONTENTS

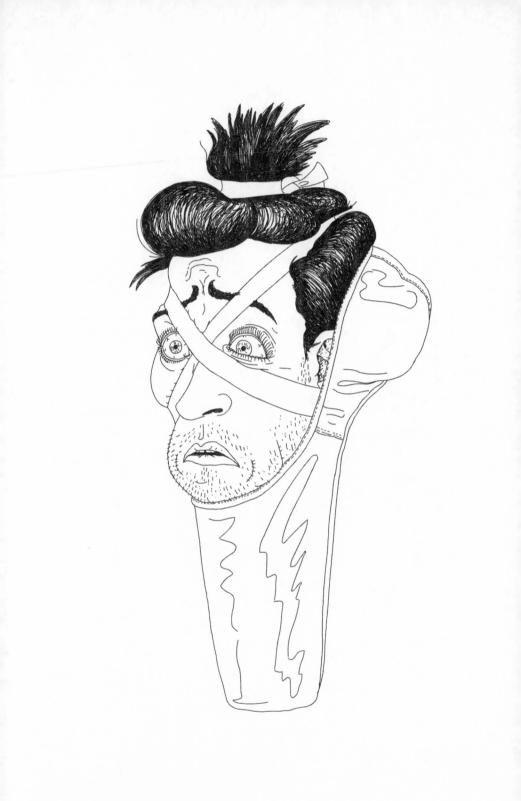

Dear Reader,

There's a mark on every stage around the world that signifies the center of its depth and width, called "center center." Since I was twelve years old, I have dreamed of standing on that very mark as a principal dancer with the illustrious American Ballet Theatre at the Metropolitan Opera House at New York City's Lincoln Center. This absurd, nonchronological collection of essays tells the story of how I got there, from the inevitable coming-out story to the evolution of my career to fantastical run-ins with Jesus Christ on Grindr.

I always knew I wanted to write a book. In true delusional form, I had given it the title *Center Center* when I was around twenty years old, a good fifteen years before writing the damned thing. Talk about putting the cart before the horse. When an editor at Penguin contacted me in 2019 and asked coolly, "Have you ever considered writing a book?" I nearly fainted.

A New Yorker is always busy, so my first task was to set aside a chunk of time to write. I asked my boss, American Ballet Theatre artistic director Kevin McKenzie, if I could skip *The Nutcracker* during the 2019 season, and he obliged. My friends Nate and Peter offered their uninhabited upstate cottage to me. I packed my coziest sweatpants and took the Amtrak up to Rhinecliff, where I sat in an unfinished kitchen in the dead of winter, without heat, while it snowed foot upon foot. Gazing out onto the frozen pond, I wrote tales of denial, ambiguous relationships with male friends, wronged girlfriends, major setbacks and triumphs in ballet, and death in the family. The memories in this book all meet at a crossroads with self-awareness, acceptance, irony, friendship, love, and sex. The honesty with which I present myself has come at a high price, paid in life experiences. Each essay in this collection will shock (some are rather NC-17), amuse, embolden, and inspire.

At thirty-seven, I have realized my childhood dream. What, if anything, is left? Let's find out together, standing under the dusty spotlight on CENTER CENTER.

Merde! (as they say),
James Whiteside

CENTER
CENTER

GETTING YOUR DREAM JOB IS AS EASY AS ABT

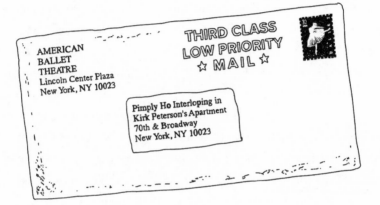

AMERICAN
BALLET
THEATRE
Lincoln Center Plaza
New York, NY 10023

THIRD CLASS
LOW PRIORITY
☆ MAIL ☆

Pimply Ho Interloping in
Kirk Peterson's Apartment
70th & Broadway
New York, NY 10023

I was twelve when my first dance teachers, Angie and Steve, took me to New York City's famed Lincoln Center to see an American Ballet Theatre performance. It was early spring in 1996. The Twin Towers still stood, the premiere of *Sex and the City* was on the horizon, and the outrageous gentrification of New York City's grimiest neighborhoods had yet to occur. It was a magical time for the world's most vivaciously vicious city.

ABT's spring gala is structured like a "greatest hits" show. It's chock-full of excerpted scenes from the company's most famous ballets: *Swan Lake*, *Don Quixote*, and *Romeo and Juliet*, as well as American classics by Twyla Tharp, Agnes de Mille, Antony Tudor, and Mark Morris. The spring gala is the easiest way to understand why ABT is the most prestigious classical ballet company in the United States and why Congress declared it "America's National Ballet Company." I was struggling with ballet at the time and much preferred my tap and jazz classes. At that age, dancing to Janet Jackson is preferable to dancing to canned piano ballet class music via cassette tape. But my teachers knew I had potential in ballet, so they took me to the show in an attempt to inspire me. In those pre-YouTube days, I had no access to videos of great ballet dancers, nor could I follow my favorite dancers on Instagram. There was no Googling of Rudolf Nureyev or Mikhail Baryshnikov. I was a ballet ignoramus.

It was the first time I saw what ballet *could* be. I watched that ABT gala performance the way a Pop Warner football player watches the Super Bowl. As a child with a flair for the absurdly theatrical, I was struck by the show's obvious glamour. I also witnessed men in tights for the first time. I recall thinking, "What on earth is going on in there?!" Like many of my earliest homosexual inclinations, I mistook my attraction for simple curiosity. I was blown away by the performance: the virtuosity, the music, the costumes, the drama, THE BUTTS!

Angie and Steve had an old friend named Kirk Peterson who was an ABT ballet master (a coach), and they took me backstage to say hello. A towering security guard with a clipboard of names let us through to the dressing rooms, where the floor transformed from utilitarian tile to luxurious red carpeting, and the lighting eased into a soft, incandescent ambiance. Next to some red velvet sofas was a small table with dozens of filled champagne flutes, ripe for the picking. Dressers (theater staff who assist with getting artists in and out of very intricate costumes) milled about, hanging costumes to dry and gathering dirty bags of laundry. Ballerinas ghosted around in long silk kimonos and house slippers, talking to each other while taking down their beautifully braided updos. Male dancers laughed and homoerotically jostled each other, wearing nothing but their tights and suspenders; some were even drinking sweaty beers. I think it is still the sexiest place I've ever been.

"Where are we?" I asked, with the awe of someone witnessing the rapture.

"The Principal Hallway, darling," Angie replied in her British accent. We had successfully infiltrated the sacred dressing grounds of ABT's star dancers.

I thought to myself, "This will be my home one day."

WHEN YOU'RE A young ballet student, "Where do you summer?" does not mean "Where are your myriad vacation homes?" Many dance schools in cities and towns the world over house summer programs. Angie and Steve suggested I audition for ABT's Summer Intensive in the year 2000, when I was fifteen. What a time to be a teenager! I auditioned and received a full scholarship to the program. I believe my teachers pulled some strings with their friends at ABT to ensure I could go. My family had zero extra income for summer dance camps, which can cost thousands of dollars.

I commuted every day from Fairfield, Connecticut, to Union Square in New York City, where ABT's studios are located, because my mother would not let me live alone in the city for the summer. It was a long commute, but it was perhaps my favorite part of the day. I'd board the Metro-North train with my dance bag, my Discman, a sleeve of CDs, and a notebook. It was never overcrowded in those times and I always found a seat. There are too many goddamned people in the world now. I'd settle into the maroon-and-beige vinyl seats, pop in a Fiona Apple or Ani DiFranco album, and write poetry or journal for an hour and a half, fueled by teenage angst and hormones. Most of my journal entries began with homosexual curiosity and ended in guilt-ridden heterosexual cover-ups. I wrote as though I was sure my journal was going to be discovered and published someday. I've always been a champ at delusion.

I was placed in the third-lowest level, Blue, out of ten levels at the ABT Summer Intensive. I quickly became very aware that I was not as refined a dancer as many of the star students. Ballet's young prodigies all went to ABT's summer program in hopes of getting into ABT Studio Company, ABT's apprentice company. There was a performance at the end of the program in which excerpts of various classical ballets were performed for a paying audience. It served as a capitalist scheme (rich parents, bwah-ha-ha!) as well as an audition for the Studio Company. I didn't have a hope in hell. My first year, I danced a crunchy modern piece in culottes—there was no way they'd let me near classical ballet. I was not offered a place in the Studio Company. No surprise there.

That first year, I was not yet out of the closet, even though I had been hooking up with my two best friends in Connecticut, Kurt and Jordan, for years. However, I was aware of my attraction to guys. There was a short, fifteen-year-old Latino boy named Julian at ABT who fascinated me. He was a native New Yorker, cussed up a storm, and had a very developed body. I was drawn to his muscled physique and gruff demeanor. Julian defined himself as bisexual. We had a sleepover at his New York apartment, and he talked to me about his girlfriend. "We can't hook up because I'm in a relationship," he whispered, inches from my face, "but we can cuddle." So we cuddled through the night and our boners threatened to spontaneously combust.

Throughout the ABT Summer Intensive, I was awed and inspired not only by the dancers of the main company, but also by my fellow students. They were well-trained, disciplined, lithe creatures who barreled through the technically difficult combinations. Each ballet class was a fresh competition in which students tried to prove why they should be a part of the main company. Every glimpse of the elusive artists of American Ballet Theatre incentivized young dancers to reach for the stars and work just that much harder. Paloma Herrera, an Argentine prima ballerina, stalked the hallways icily, always diligently setting to her task of being the consummate professional and artist. Stunned students stood speechless, pressed against the walls of the narrow, grimy halls. Julie Kent, ABT's reigning American prima, sweetly smized in the general direction of aspiring ballerinas, as if to say, "Good luck, girls."

I wasn't just smitten with ballet, I was in love with the *idea* of ABT. After my first year at the Summer Intensive, I went back to my dance school in Fairfield and continued my training with Angie and Steve. They tried their hardest to get me into ABT's Studio Company, driving me into the city multiple times to take class with ABT, to no avail. I must've casually auditioned for Studio Company three or more times! WHY WON'T YOU LOVE ME BACK?!?!?!?!?!

THE FOLLOWING YEAR, I reauditioned for ABT's Summer Intensive and was awarded another full scholarship, I imagine thanks to my teachers' having pulled some strings for me again. They had also arranged an apartment in New York City for me, as one of their friends—Kirk Peterson, the coach we had visited backstage at the spring gala four years before—was away for the summer and needed a house sitter.

Culturally, the summer of 2001 was incredible. I was sixteen, freshly out of the closet, and living alone at Kirk Peterson's abandoned studio apartment on Seventieth and Broadway. I shuffled around the parquet floors of my apartment to newly released hits by Missy Elliott ("Get Ur Freak On"), *NSYNC ("Pop"), and Alicia Keys ("Fallin'"), and screamed along to my purchased-on-the-street bootleg *Moulin Rouge* soundtrack. I discovered Harry Potter and read the books with religious fervor. I lived across the street from a twenty-four-hour McDonald's and frequently rode the then 1/9 train with a fistful of french fries. A splendorous time, indeed.

Ballet proved to be an elusive muse. Much to my chagrin, I was placed in Blue Level for the second year in a row, while many of my peers from the previous year moved up a few levels, some even to the highest level. Several of my now-contemporaries were in the program with me: Misty Copeland, David Hallberg, and many more. They were of course in the highest level and had already been offered contracts with ABT Studio Company. I couldn't even be jealous . . . they were that much better than me.

I befriended two people in particular that year, one in my level and one in the highest level. Blaine Hoven, now an ABT soloist, and I were both in Blue Level for two consecutive years. The two of us were considered *jazzerinas*, which is a demeaning term for dancers trained predominantly in jazz. At the time, Blaine was a roly-poly, in-the-closet Southern queen from Alabama. We laughed and joked constantly and still do. Our other friend, Simone Messmer, was in the highest level. She was white as snow, bone-thin, smoked like a chimney, and had the maroon dye job of an Eastern European babushka. I found her terribly glamorous; her cutting remarks illuminated my world. She'd often stand outside my building in a large sun hat (she loathed the sun) while balancing on demi-pointe in arabesque, puffing away at a Marlboro Light 100, her vampire-burgundy lipstick staining the filter. Blaine, Simone, and I were inseparable.

I recall very little of my actual ballet training that summer. The social frontiers were too vast to allocate brain space to it. Post-coming-out, I began to dress like some sort of homosexual rebel, with glitter-embedded JNCO jeans and crop tops. I wore my hair gelled into eight to ten spikes and had my tongue pierced with a royal-blue marble barbell. I enjoyed the cystic acne of youth and went through puberty in earnest. I was rather revolting.

Regardless, my social life was booming. One night I had a fabulous party at my (Kirk's) apartment, where I invited loads of other dancers over to drink copious amounts of mixed liquors. There was gin, vodka, sangria, champagne, beer, and Mike's Hard Lemonade. There was also no shortage of marijuana. I fancied myself a stoner at the time. I don't know where we got all the booze from, as we were all surely under twenty-one, but it was there nevertheless. We got hammered and danced all night. We danced on the bed, which was actually just a pull-out sofa, to Missy Elliott's "4 My People." As we jumped up and down shouting the lyrics, we heard a loud crack and fell through the iron frame of the sofa bed, which had bent and twisted like there'd been an earthquake.

In the middle of the night, we decided to go to Times Square. We picked up six-packs of beer and stopped at the Forty-Second Street McDonald's. A dozen wasted teenagers, belligerently ordering cheese-burgers at three a.m. before going to Central Park to smoke blunts and drink champagne straight from the bottle. Beautiful and horrible. I don't know who funded this whole excursion, but it sure wasn't me. The park was dark and terrifying, but we were oblivious and very lucky. We encountered no one—mugger, police, or otherwise.

Someone had brought a friend along, a gay student from a city college. He was tall, with a nerdy posture that said, "I love my Yahoo! email address!!!" His hair had frosted tips, and he wore a white button-down with an ashy-green knit sweater vest on top and thick, black-rimmed, rectangular glasses. He was vaguely attractive, and I was a drunk, horny teenager. The two of us left the park and went back to the now-broken sofa bed in my apartment, where I proceeded to drunkenly bat his half-hard penis around like a cat lazily swatting at a paralyzed mouse. I never told Kirk that I destroyed his sofa bed.

The Summer Intensive again came to a close with a performance. For the second year in a row, I was not allowed to do classical ballet, and was made instead to do a flamenco dance that was essentially a competition jazz number. I watched from the sidelines as Misty Copeland and David Hallberg danced their classical repertoire. They were elegant and serious, or at least appeared so. Their technical proficiency and finesse were miles away from anything I was capable of, making me feel like a bedazzled turd. Why couldn't I be like them, taking the obvious next steps to achieve their dreams?

There were two options here: pity myself or do better. That night was a turning point for me. It was a breezy New York City summer night, and Simone and I were perched on the roof of my brick apartment building like angsty teenage gargoyles. As I performatively smoked a Marlboro Light 100, my first-ever cigarette, I vowed to improve at ballet—to become one of the Misty Copelands or David Hallbergs of the world.

"Good luck, honey," Simone chuckled, her witchy, pointed face and my pockmarked, fuzzy cheeks illuminated by a hazy Gotham City moon.

I KNEW I NEEDED TO improve in ballet, and by that point, I truly wanted to. I had languished in Blue Level for two years and had been cut after the first of three rounds in the Youth America Grand Prix finals in New York City. I had some catching up to do.

My childhood friend Kurt went to a boarding school called North Carolina School of the Arts and suggested I send audition materials. I tried, but didn't get in. Many people had suggested I audition for New York City Ballet's School of American Ballet, but I had heard that many of the dancers were wayward souls like me, and I was trying to reform myself from an apathetic jazzerina pothead to a focused, studious bunhead. Finally, I sent my audition materials to another

Southern school called Virginia School of the Arts and was accepted with a full scholarship.

Alone, at seventeen, I boarded a commercial plane that seated ten and flew to my new home: Lynchburg, Virginia. That any town in the South continues to be called *Lynchburg* boggles my mind. The headmaster of the school was a former Royal Ballet principal dancer named Petrus Bosman. He was a cheeky old British homosexual who wore an incredible toupee, thick, clear-framed glasses, and a white buttondown tucked into high-waisted light-denim jeans. He loved musicals and made us watch dance scenes from them during class. One of my first performances at the school was a recreation of Bob Fosse's "Steam Heat" from *The Pajama Game.*

My main teacher was named David Keener, another older homosexual who proudly flew a pride flag in front of his Southern colonial house. Every single day, he worked tirelessly with me on my ballet technique. One day during ballet class, we were all balancing on demi-pointe on one leg at the barre when my ankle gave out and I fell. Mr. Keener rushed over to me and began stomping at the floor, shouting, "Damn those fairies! Did they trip you? I'll get them! Goddamn those fairies!!!" I erupted into laughter, as did the rest of the class, and then we got back to work.

That was how much of the year went. I knew I had catching up to do, but the staff believed in me and saw I had the will of a warrior. I worked my fucking ass off to improve that year.

When I went home to Connecticut for Christmas, I discovered a letter (a real paper letter with a stamp on it!) from American Ballet Theatre. I voraciously tore it open and read:

Dear Mr. James Whiteside,

We regret to inform you that we will not be offering you another full scholarship to the ABT Summer Intensive. We hope you understand. If you wish to attend, you must reaudition. If accepted, you will be required to pay full tuition.

> *Sincerely,*
> *The ABT Education Department*

The letter might as well have said:

Dear Fuckface,

You squandered two years of opportunity. You'll be lucky if you get into Dolly Dinkle Dance Company. We can't believe you broke Kirk Peterson's bed. You little garbage diaper. At least you got some sloppy D though! I bet that's what you're thinking, you little shit person. You're welcome to audition again, but you won't get in, and you know it. BWAH-HA-HA-HA-HA!!!!!!!!

> *Eat a dick,*
> *Bowser*

I crumpled up the letter and vowed to get revenge. It was essentially like vowing to get revenge on myself, as I was the dumbass who had squandered my own chances.

When I returned to Lynchburg, I worked even harder than when I had first arrived. I showed up early to class and stayed late afterward. I still wasn't the best dancer there, but at least I was trying to be.

With the ABT Summer Intensive out of the question, I was forced to audition elsewhere. Audition season is a marathon of harshly judged ballet classes. Each audition comes with a fee, naturally. Unfortunately, I was on my own this time. I didn't have my teachers pulling any strings for me. I auditioned for Houston Ballet's Summer Intensive, and they said that when I finished school, they would offer me a corps de ballet contract. This was the first sign that I was on the right track and that my ballet technique was improving. The second sign was that when I auditioned for Boston Ballet's Summer Dance Program, I was accepted with a full scholarship. Things were looking up.

I chose Boston over Houston because I was scared of homophobic Texans. (Little did I know that there were plenty of homophobic Bostonians as well.) That summer I packed up and moved into a Boston University dorm, where the Summer Dance Program attendees were housed, for six weeks. In stark contrast with my summers at ABT, I don't recall making any real friends in the program, and instead retreated into my training. I was placed in the highest of two men's levels. It was the first time I'd been placed in the highest level. Even though there were only two, I considered it an accomplishment. For the end-of-program performance, I was cast as one of the side couples in the pas d'action from *La Bayadère*. This also marked the first time I was cast to do classical ballet in a final performance.

Immediately after the performance, Boston Ballet's director, Mikko Nissinen, offered the lead dancer of *La Bayadère* a contract in Boston Ballet II, the apprentice company. He declined, so Mikko offered it to another dancer. He also declined. Finally, at the behest of BBII director Raymond Lukens, one of my career's guardian angels, the final contract was awarded to me. Stunned, I called my mother and told her, "I don't think I'm ready. I need more training."

"If not now . . . when?" she asked.

I JOINED BBII in September of 2002, at eighteen years old. I loved being a professional. I was finally in charge of my own fate. I worked hard, studied those who were better dancers than me, and improved. I went from last kid picked in gym class to new kid on the block.

At the end of the year, three things can happen: you can get fired, you can get rehired as an apprentice, or you can get promoted to corps de ballet in the main company. I was offered another year of apprenticeship in BBII, which was exactly what I had expected. But a week before the new season started, I received a message on my answering machine from Mikko's assistant, Liz. I called her back and she said, "How would you like to be in the corps de ballet?"

I was gobsmacked. Apparently, a French guy Mikko had hired had failed to get his work visa, so there was an extra contract available. I shouted, "YES! A THOUSAND TIMES YES!!!" as if I were being proposed to by the crown prince of Genovia.

In December 2011, Raymond Lukens called me on my iPhone 3G. I had been at Boston Ballet for ten years by then, moving all the way through the ranks from apprentice to principal dancer. He left me a message that said, "It's time for you to audition for ABT. They need men."

Audition materials consist of a headshot, a résumé, and a video of one's dancing. I sent them to the email address Raymond had given me and received a prompt reply requesting that I come take company ballet class, which happens daily. As I was in the middle of an arduous run of *Nutcracker* performances, I had only Mondays off. I'd have to zip down to New York City to audition and zoop back up to Boston the next day to do more performances.

I took the now-defunct Fung Wah Bus service from Boston's Chinatown to NYC's Chinatown after a Sunday matinee performance of *The Nutcracker*, dozing off in the narrow, prickly-yet-fuzzy bus seat. I got in well after two a.m. and crashed on my brother Robbie's couch on the Lower East Side. After a few hours of sleep, I got up, primped, and made my way over to Union Square for an audition that would drastically change my life.

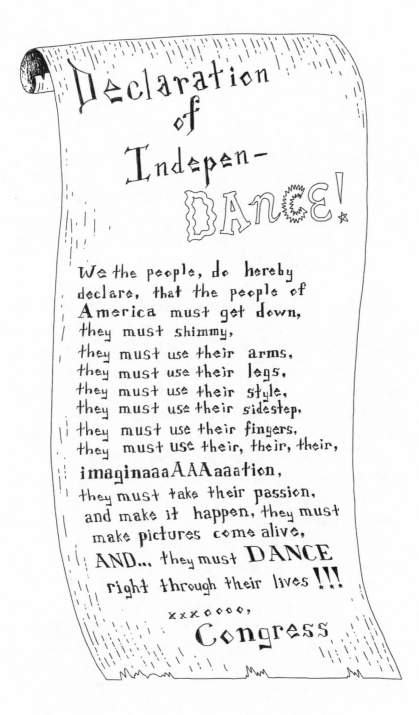

Feeling like the prodigal son, I reentered the stomping grounds of my youth: 890 Broadway, ABT Studios. A wave of youthful nostalgia washed over me. The old New Yorkiness of the architecture. The scent of sweat. The piano sounds pervading every crevice. It was a strange sensation, and I was nervous.

At twenty-eight, I had ten years of professional dancing under my belt. I knew what it was like when auditioners came to take class with a company. I felt like an inconvenience, so I stayed off to the side of the room. One by one, dancers filed in. I recognized many of them as the stars of ABT: Julie Kent, Gillian Murphy, Paloma Herrera, Marcelo Gomes, Roberto Bolle, and more. I also had some old friends in the class, like Blaine and Simone!

The class was much easier than the classes in Boston Ballet and I felt excellent, executing the simple combinations with confidence. ABT artistic director Kevin McKenzie watched about five to ten minutes of the class. I was sure he wasn't interested, because he'd watched so little of my audition, but his associate artistic director, Victor Barbee, had watched nearly the whole thing. He must've put in a good word, because when the class ended, Kevin's assistant asked me to come upstairs for a meeting.

I was sent into the associate director's office, where Kevin and Victor were seated, waiting for me. They told me to sit down opposite them. I was sweating and visibly anxious. My fate rested in these space-time-dilated moments.

"We think you'd fit in nicely here at ABT and we'd like to offer you a soloist contract," Kevin said.

I nearly had a heart attack, and my butthole practically imploded. "Th-that's incredible," I managed to stutter. "Th-th-thank you!"

"Welcome to ABT," Kevin and Victor said with genial smiles, as I shook their hands and shuffled out of the office in stunned silence.

I walked to a nearby deli and sat at the grimy bar in the window, looking out at the frenetic New York City streets, thinking, "This will be my home. This was always supposed to be my home."

But two weeks later, a few hours before another *Nut* performance, Kevin called me. "Listen, James. I've got to be honest with you," he said. "You coming in as a soloist is really going to hurt morale, and I can't have that. I'm very sorry but I'd like to offer you a corps de ballet contract. Just come in and do some group dances and sword fights and then I'll promote you."

To clarify, principal dancer is the highest rank, then soloist, then corps de ballet. I was all right with taking a step down from principal at Boston Ballet to soloist at ABT because it was my dream company and the largest and most prestigious in the country. But to step down two ranks to corps? I was speechless. I wasn't affronted so much as disappointed. "I should've known it was too good to be true," I thought to myself. I understood his rationale. There were a lot of young up-and-comers already in ABT vying for the rank of soloist. Why the hell should this sassy cat from Boston get it? What people didn't know was that I'd been striving for this position since I was twelve years old, and that I'd never given up on it. I had been a principal dancer in Boston for three years before auditioning for ABT. To go from being a happy principal dancer all the way back to the corps de ballet sounded agonizing. All that work! Just to start all over again! I said, "I'll think about it overnight and I'll call you back tomorrow."

I barely slept that night. So many questions careened about in my head. Would he actually promote me? Would I ever be a principal again? Would my boyfriend come with me? Would I like it there? Would I make any friends as good as the friends I had in Boston?

The next morning, I called him back. "I'm sorry, Kevin, but I can't do it," I told him. "I can't go backwards. I hope you understand. Thank you, though."

"I understand," he said. "Thank you and good luck," and then he hung up. I sat there numb, wondering if I'd just made the biggest mistake of my life.

A few minutes later, my phone buzzed. It was Kevin again.

"OK," he said, when I answered the phone. "Soloist it is."

My skin tingled. My hair stood on end, like in a Japanese anime. My eyes watered and I was practically vibrating with effusive joy. Has joy ever affected you so much that you can sense your biological humanness? I felt my skin flush, my heart swell and shudder, each hair follicle prickle. I thanked him profusely, not masking the emotion in my voice, and said I would not disappoint him.

ENTERING THE Metropolitan Opera House backstage area in September of 2012, the first time in sixteen years, was a definitive moment for me—a moment I had waited a long time for. I arrived early in the morning, with a small suitcase filled with my theater things. I had my headphones in and was listening to my *Glee* playlist on shuffle. As I entered the stage door, a beautiful Andrew Lloyd Webber song came on: "As If We Never Said Goodbye." I was walking into the house of my dreams, the house I had vowed to live in when I was only twelve years old.

As I made my way down the hallway to the dressing rooms with silent tears springing to my eyes, I dragged my free hand along the walls and envisioned myself as the delusional Norma Desmond from *Sunset Boulevard*, desperately returning to the glittering scenes of her youth. The difference was that my future was still ahead of me, mine to mold. I realized I was being insane and quickly reeled it in lest anyone see me weeping and twirling along the linoleum hallways, dragging a cheap suitcase behind me.

I turned a corner and was confronted by the scene of my twelve-year-old youth: the Principal Hallway. It looked smaller, duller, and more accessible than I had remembered it, but still it wasn't at all disappointing, with the morning light streaming in sideways from Amsterdam Avenue through thin black blinds. As a soloist, I didn't yet have access to that prestigious Principal Hallway—but seeing it again, I knew that, at last, I was home, and that I would stop at nothing to get my very own principal dressing room.

JBDUBS & ÜHU BETCH

"You need to butch it up." "You're running like a girl." "Don't wear that headband. You're not a ballerina." "That color is too bright." "Don't open your eyes so much. You look like a woman." "Don't move so quickly. Only ladies move that quickly."

The gulf between man and woman is deep in the world of classical ballet. The stories simply don't allow for much variation, unless you're some sort of mincing villain. I thought that by becoming a ballet dancer, I was doing something super gay, but it turns out my life's work is just another heteronormative endeavor. Prince Siegfried in *Swan Lake*: straight. Prince Albrecht in *Giselle*: straight. Prince Désiré in *The Sleeping Beauty*: straight. How can one be heterosexual with a name like Prince Désiré?! It sounds like it's straight off the plot synopsis of a 1995 Falcon Studios VHS porno tape:

> *Jeff the Big-Dick Trucker fell asleep for one hundred years at the Sunoco off I-95. His boner grew and grew until Prince Désiré discovered and awakened him by kissing his sleeping cock. Jeff the Big-Dick Trucker had been asleep for one hundred years! His truck was completely full and it was way past due to deliver his load. Thank goodness for Prince Désiré!*

One of my former bosses once told me that I didn't get the part of Romeo because I was wearing a headband for technique class. I thought I'd tear my hair out. How can such an elegant, exquisite art form be so blatantly homophobic?

I think that so many queer people become luminary creatives because during our youths, we were forced to be imaginative in how we existed. Upon realizing that I didn't fit into the societal norm and therefore couldn't fall back on the easiest and most obvious definitions of *success*, I found ways to make myself seen and heard. I believe normalcy to be an insidious evil, one that leaves you slowly shuffling down the path millions have taken before you. While being queer itself is already like taking a road less traveled, it's what you do on that road that defines you—not the queerness.

I wasn't able to express my true self in my art, for which I have worked my *entire* life. *Who am I and what do I want to say?* Every single role I play is heterosexual. *Every single one.* How could someone as gay as me be forced into heterosexual submission so often? Think of my gayness like Jeff the Big-Dick Trucker's load. It had been neglected for far too long.

If I didn't make some gay roles for myself, who would?

Thus, my alter egos were born: JbDubs, the pop musician, and

Ühu Betch, the drag queen with a flair for nonsense. Both gay. Both proud. Both camp as Christmas.

THE BIRTH OF JBDUBS:
OUT-AND-PROUD POP MUSICIAN

Music has always been the reason I dance. I have willingly let it manipulate my soul and body. I have encouraged its machinations and worshipped at its omnipotent altar.

The first CD I ever owned was *Jagged Little Pill* by Alanis Morissette, followed by Toni Braxton's *Secrets* and then George Michael's *Older.* As you can imagine, I quickly discovered that I deeply identified as a vengeful white woman; a sexy, Black, androgynous chanteuse; and a Grammy Award–winning homosexual connoisseur of cruising.

A few years later, during my train commutes from Connecticut to my first ABT summer program in New York City, I listened obsessively to two albums that curated or perhaps birthed my emo poet mystique: *Tidal* and *When the Pawn . . .* , both by Fiona Apple. I'd blast Miss Apple on my Discman and write poetry that almost always centered around unrequited love or my failed attempts at turning straight boys into homosexuals.

Missy Elliott's staccato rap inspired me to inspect more closely the relationship between music and lyrics, and her longtime production collaborator, Timbaland, blew my mind. I'd take the train into the city and make a beeline to Virgin Megastore in Times Square, where I'd rotate through the listening stations in hopes of finding "the sound." Production became as important as the artist herself. (I listened almost exclusively to women, with the exception of *NSYNC, who were basically primped pageant queens anyway.)

In 2005, when I turned twenty-one, I used my hard-earned wages to purchase what would become my most prized possession: an Apple iMac G5. I had been working professionally since 2002, and this was the first truly expensive thing I had ever bought. The computer came equipped with GarageBand, a rudimentary music production program and my gateway drug to becoming a self-taught digital musician.

I set myself to my task. I would create a sonic masterpiece, one for the ages. It would be my legacy. It would be sent forth on extraterrestrial messaging missions. It would show that the human race is prodigious, just, and luminous. My work would be installed as a preloaded MP3 on all iPods henceforth!

I toyed with music loops (prerecorded beats and melodies). I reached for my notepad and scribbled out the lyrics to my first number-one smash: "Fat-Ass Bitch."

Incredible how creations mimic the emotional intelligence of their creators. I knew that by making a joke of my work, I couldn't/wouldn't be forced to be taken seriously. This has been a defense mechanism my whole life, to keep judgment at arm's length. If I truly show my honest vulnerability in my work, I will be fully visible. At twenty-one, I was not yet ready to do such a thing.

It's frustrating, this complete dedication to self-preservation. I am a pretend person. I am a laughing Band-Aid.

I became obsessed with writing and producing music, and I decided I wanted to perform as my pop-star alter ego, JbDubs. *J* for James. *B* for Bruce. *Dubs* for the *W* in Whiteside. My friends and I frequented a club in Boston called Machine, and on one belligerent evening out, I handed DJ Susan my homemade mixtape. She begrudgingly accepted it. Handing your mixtape to a DJ named Susan is probably not the best course of action. What's next? DJ *Ethel?* DJ *Muriel?* In my mind, this is how it all played out:

Damn, I looked good. I was wearing my whisker-marked, sand-blasted, boot-cut H&M jeans over my puffiest Marshalls-bought, ambiguously branded sneakers. I had scissored a secondhand Urban Outfitters tee to veritable nipple pasties, and my twink-like, emaciated horse frame shone in the almost-chic Boston nightclub disco lights. I clutched my burned disc, packed in a slim neon case in my right hand, my fingernails bitten to uneven and jagged nubs. I confidently leaned over the DJ deck and shouted over the pulsating throb of "Don't Cha" by the Pussycat Dolls. "Hey, DJ Susan!" I screamed. "Here's that mixtape you've been spamming my Myspace for."

The following week, I returned and asked if she'd listened to it. She said that she had and that she'd enjoyed it, so she'd ask the promoter if I could perform at any of his clubs. The promoter's name was Rafael, and he was a corpulent gentleman with a cheery disposition, at complete odds with the title *club promoter.* He decided I needed to do an out-of-town audition for the chance to perform in any Boston clubs. As it is known across the globe, Boston is the absolute pinnacle of the clubbing experience.

That is how my best friends and I ended up in Manchester, New Hampshire, a small city with a population of around one hundred thousand. I rented a car and forced my friends to be my backup dancers. This is something I would become infamous for: getting my friends to do embarrassing things for absolutely zero money. By this point, I had been dating Dan (aka Milk) for over a year, and he had transformed from a reticent femme to a full-blown drag queen. I enlisted him to be my drag-queen-in-residence and essentially hand me props while I sang and danced.

When we arrived in Manchester, we checked in to the scuzzy Econo Lodge off the highway. All costs were paid out of pocket, as this was MY BIG BREAK! We fastidiously rehearsed our choreography as if we were doing solos in the Olympics' Opening Ceremony. Milk was getting into makeup in the bathroom, ensuring that he would look like Mrs. Potato Head, when there was a horrifying, violent pounding on the door. I opened it to find a large man standing there, brandishing an ax.

"I'm a firefighter. Stay in your room. There's a hostage situation in the room next door. They could be violent. We're going in."

We gay-gasped in terror and shut the door. "But what do we do if nobody is caught or dead by the time we need to leave for the club?!" I asked in a panicked whisper.

Fortunately, the suspect was neutralized, and our very first JbDubs show went swimmingly. We shimmied around the houseplants littering the triangular, foot-high mezzanine that constituted a stage. We danced with vigor and gusto, and I sang with my usual rhythmically atonal, slightly deaf-sounding zeal. A rousing success indeed.

When I finally got the opportunity to perform in Boston, it was bittersweet. The young gays did not come out to hear me "sing"; they came out to dance, drink, and hook up with strangers. Every time I'd appear onstage, it was to break up a night of dancing.

Performing for an audience who wanted nothing to do with me had no deterring effect on me, though. I'd have been happy performing my music to a beach full of seagulls. I'd much rather create something no one wants anything to do with than not create anything at all.

Not only did I want to perform, I also wanted to make albums and music videos. For the lead single on my sophomore album, *Oink*, I dreamed up a "Single Ladies"–esque music video starring myself and my two best friends, Mack and Lola, as disgruntled gay office workers. We covered the back of Boston Ballet's basement studio in white photo paper on a lazy Sunday morning and dressed ourselves in five-dollar white H&M button-downs, black ties, black booty shorts, and cherry-red high heels. We filmed the video in a few exhausting hours and titled it "I Hate My Job."

When it was finished, I scheduled a release party at our favorite bar and invited all my friends. It went live on YouTube that night and rapidly made its way onto Facebook profiles all over the world. The thing I had dreamed up and executed had been deemed a viral hit by the masses! Overnight, I had gone from a fantasy pop singer to someone the public believed was a real, live pop singer.

UPON SCROLLING THROUGH the comments on the YouTube video for "I Hate My Job" one day, I discovered the following words: *hate speech, slur, transphobic, bigot.* Here are the lyrics they were referring to:

As I walk by, I get a pat on the fanny
Don't look at me like I'm a two-dollar tranny

A word I had been using with jovial delight was being called out as hate speech. I was shaken by the negative attention and didn't know what to do. Even though I didn't consider myself transphobic, I had still been using the t-word willy-nilly for years, with ignorance as my only defense. But one can plead ignorance for only so long.

I, as a sensible human being, wish solely to support and uplift the queer community, so I quickly issued a Twitter apology. A Twitter apology does not negate one's error. The song remains in its original state containing the offensive lyric. It is a reminder that I mustn't relinquish my mind to comfort, to perpetual sameness.

I have learned from my missteps, and I continue to educate myself. My awakenings were a direct result of people informing me when I shared insensitive creations. I have gained wisdom from my shame.

I once went to a cute Brooklyn garden party at which I met someone from New York City Ballet. He was waxing on in a nasal baritone about the *films* he'd seen lately and how they were all *laden with inherent*

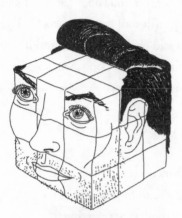
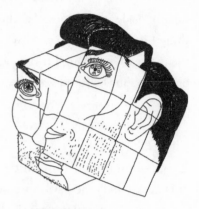
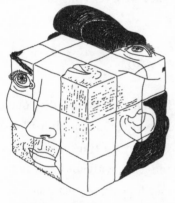
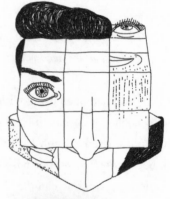

homophobia and misogyny. Afterward, I giggled about it with my boy-friend and commented that the people at the party were the most pretentious I'd ever met. The truth was, the nasal NYCB dancer was probably right; I just didn't have enough perspective to hear his words properly. The ignorant find a way to revel in their ignorance, to cele-brate it and defend it to the idiotic end. While I pride myself on avoid-ing pretentiousness, at which point am I an imbecile with my hands clapped over my ears in blatant refusal to hear honest truths? I strive to someday find the balance.

I'm grateful to have learned a lot since the writing of "I Hate My Job," which remains my most popular song to date. Ignorance is not bliss, it's hell. Knowledge is bliss.

Making music has allowed me to live a fantasy life alongside my real life. I don't think I'll ever stop writing and producing. I don't yet have a therapist, so when something shakes me or I need to expel a feeling, it goes into a song, simple as that. If I'm lonely, or full of rage, or confused, or jealous, or silly, or incredulous, it finds its way into my microphone and out of my head. Creativity and expression *are* cathar-sis. If I were to shut myself up and silence my voice, I'd wither. I wouldn't die, but I'd languish till I was indistinguishable from any-body else. Who you are is how you think and what you choose to do with those thoughts. No one has the power to tell you who you are, but you have the choice to give yourself the freedom to explore who you are through expression. What do *you* want to say?

ÜHU BETCH: A DRAG QUEEN ORIGIN STORY

Let's go back in time. My first forays into drag took place around the same time I bought that first iMac G5. While I happily danced my way up through the ranks of Boston Ballet, I made some unbelievable friends who shaped the way I thought about self-expression. Everyone was always making things and sharing them with each other. This was before Instagram, so people were doing things they wanted without worrying about garnering Likes. I lived with my friends in what could surely be called a gay frat house. Because we were and still are all raging homosexuals, we called it "the Homosexuals' Home," which was later abbreviated to "the Homes' Home," and then simply "the Homes." It's not at all ironic that it sounds like some sort of halfway house.

My friend Lucas, a Vietnamese American ballet dancer from California, had already been showing up in drag at company house parties as a provocative prostitute named Vixie. As Vixie, Lucas was a hilariously clumsy parody of a woman. It was an honest representation of a gay man's obsession with all things *woman.*

My other drag queen roommates were Tony as Nicoteena Patch, aka Teena, and Mack as Fefe. My ex-boyfriend Dan, as Giselle Peacock, was a later addition. Nicoteena prided herself on how much she looked like an adorable little girl, and Fefe satisfied herself by being the group's resident "messy queen" (though in my opinion, Fefe's antics almost always outshone everyone else's). I liked the idea of not having a real proper-noun kind of name, so I decided upon That Girl, after the 1960s sitcom starring Marlo Thomas.

Vixie was the ringleader of our burgeoning drag fascination, so when she glided down the stairs in her floor-length chiffon robe lined with ostrich feathers and Lucite heels and squeaked, "OK, girls! *Ten Minute T******! You have ten minutes to get into your gear!" we had no choice but to oblige. (In our minds, the t-word was just another word for *drag queen*, which we now know is not the case. To my shame, we remained ignorant for approximately five more years.)

Ten Minute T***** was a living room lip-synch series that we filmed using my mother's JVC handheld camcorder (which I borrowed . . . forever) and uploaded to a still-youthful YouTube. (Our videos predated even the infamous "Shoes" video, in which a drag queen farcically decides which shoes to buy.) This is, to this date, some of the most fun I've ever had. It wasn't *for* anything other than the extreme desire to be silly, to shed the masculine constraints we found ourselves under daily. I was liberated in a way I had never known. Our living room drag performances parodied everything it was to be a twenty-something homosexual in a classical ballet company. It felt *good*. If you've never done anything as someone else, you're missing out. Shedding yourself to inhabit a new persona is truly illuminating.

I eventually removed all the videos from YouTube upon discovering how hideous our ignorant use of the t-word was. The annihilation of our ignorance marked the end of *TMT*'s heyday. Our group scattered, time passed, and That Girl all but perished.

THOUGH THE DAYS of living room drag shows had ended, our forays into drag continued; a common activity for our Boston friend group was to get into the most absurd drag imaginable and go to a restaurant for dinner. We didn't necessarily go out as women; we went out as subverters, challenging the self-congratulating, faux-liberal inhabitants of Boston. One evening, we went to the Cheesecake Factory. As we sat in a booth at the center of the restaurant, cackling and generally causing a scene, we decided we needed new names that would reflect our evolution. Giselle Peacock had metamorphosed into an exquisite drag queen and changed her name to Milk to reflect the near-white paleness she exhibits at all times. "Why don't we all do dairy names?" Milk said, and we giggled. Thus, the Dairy Queens were born. Mack became Juggz Au Lait, Chip became Butter, and Matt, my drag daughter with Milk, became Skim. We were always the Dairy Queens, but now we had the names to match the mood.

Skim had moved to New York City to go to New York University at the same time I had joined ABT. The Dairy Queens NYC chapter consisted of Milk, Skim, and myself under my new moniker, YooHoo, after the chocolate milk–flavored beverage, which I later learned ironically contains no liquid milk. When a product is labeled as *drink*, one might as well stay away.

One balmy summer night in New York City, we bedecked ourselves in our most aggressive drag to go to a party at the Standard Hotel. The party was called ON TOP and it was a celebration of the final vestiges of New York's Club Kid era. We wore all manner of prints—striped, polka-dotted, leopard, zebra—and called ourselves "Printcesses" for an evening. When we arrived, we skipped past the line, as costumed partygoers needed not pay nor wait in line, and took the elevator up to the faux grass rooftop. There were drag queens *everywhere*. There were goths in full Victorian regalia. There were dinosaurs, witches, poodles, monsters, strippers, go-go dancers, and a slew of completely nude guests. The partiers reveled under a full city moon, basking like Poe-esque cats in a hedonistic glow.

We behaved like maniacs, drunk on liquor and attention. We pole danced, we did splits in the grass, we posed for photos unbegrudgingly. Our antics were a hit, and we received complimentary drink tickets from the party's hosts, who wanted to encourage us to return.

A host in leather and football pads accosted us and said, "Come with me. You have to meet Susanne."

We had no idea who that was, and told the host so.

"Why you're at her fete, dears!"

Susanne Bartsch was sitting in a private area settled by only the chicest attendees, wearing nothing but a sheath of black netting and nipple pasties, her wig a series of black balls made of hair and connected by a rope. Her skin was ghostly white and her deep-set eyes were rimmed with winged liner. Her false lashes looked as though they weighed as much as she did. Her petite frame and pert breasts did nothing to betray her age. We found out later that she had been the queen of queer New York City nightlife since the 1980s.

She exclaimed, "Oh, darlings! Who *ARE* you?" I felt like we were Alice, marooned in Wonderland only to be met by a strange and wonderful querying caterpillar with breast implants.

"You've *GOT* to be at my parties. I throw the *ONLY* parties worth going to anymore! You'll be paid, of course."

We stood dumbstruck and in awe.

"Take my number. Give me a call tomorrow and we'll talk about *coin*," she told us in her thick Swiss accent, as male models swarmed around her.

We began working for Susanne frequently. I performed at her parties as JbDubs as well. We were truly installing ourselves into NYC nightlife in a most glamorous way. We didn't do any drugs; we'd just get hammered on Jack Daniel's and ginger ales and perform nonsensical bits, much to the joy of the party-loving tourists.

The Dairy Queens were a theme-heavy group. We went out as nuns, jungle animals, hillbillies, the band Kiss, schoolmarms, opera singers, Instagram profiles, bathing beauties, paper dolls, hobos, the bald Powerpuff Girls, religious deities, cleaning ladies, old ladies, pregnant ladies, and skinny ladies. Once we even went out as *life itself.* We showed up to Susanne's enormous party at Marquee as drag queen babies, diapers and all, and installed ourselves on three high podiums throughout the club. As the evening wore on, we changed from babies to sullen drag queen teens, to working professionals, to mothers, to old women, and finally to ghosts. We pulled white sheets with two eyeholes out of our bags and threw them over our bodies as the public cackled and took photographs. "BOO, BITCH!" we screamed over the din.

The photographer Magnus Hastings once photographed the Dairy Queens for his exhibition. When the exhibit debuted, he asked each of us to provide a quote to accompany the photo. As we stood for more photos at the opening party, I inspected the small plaque. It read:

ÜHU

"DRAG IS LIKE CONTROLLED SCHIZOPHRENIA. I DON'T DO DRAG TO BE ONE WOMAN, I DO DRAG TO BE EVERY WOMAN. THE PRETTY, THE UGLY, THE MORBID, THE FANCIFUL, THE GEEKY, THE FUNNY, THE ALL-FEMME. I'M EVERY WOMAN, IT'S ALL IN MEEEEEEEEE."

I thought the way he spelled my name was so strange that I'd keep it and add an umlaut for good measure. Thus, YooHoo evolved into Ühu Betch. Who knows what she'll transform into next? She's like a Pokémon that way.

AS I LOOK BACK ON my life as a drag queen, I reflect that it has always brought joy, a certain sense of being alive. Milk went on to appear on *RuPaul's Drag Race* and then *RuPaul's Drag Race All Stars* on national television, which would make him a target for online hate speech and bullying as well as moderate fame. Because of that, my view of drag has become slightly jaded, but the way drag *feels* will never change. To lip-synch and dance in an intimate club, in the company of my fellow queers who scream like no balletomane would ever dare, is a freedom I would never give up, even if it cost me my principal dancer contract. Drag stands for freedom of expression and the opportunity to shed everything you've been told to be since the fucking day you were born. I express myself to stay free and in turn feel free enough to express myself in a beautiful self-perpetuating cycle.

When I began performing as these characters, I didn't care much if anyone wanted to listen; I was just happy to be shedding a bit of the repression I'd felt. JbDubs and Ühu Betch have allowed me to stay in my lane with my ballet career while maintaining the joy of having invisible lanes on either side. Think of it as a multiverse. In each version of the universe, I'm doing something vital to my emotional survival, and each universe exists at the very same time, keeping space-time happy and balanced. I am happiest when I'm able to extend my creative tentacles reaching far and away, to strange and wonderful places. I'm grateful to have JbDubs and Ühu to visit now and again, like old, reliable friends.

I never thought anyone would see or hear of either one, but I'm grateful now to be able to share them with people—especially young people, who may feel as if they'll never be heard. Being heard has nothing to do with notoriety; it's about feeling like you've a right to *exist.* And if you're asking, "What's the big deal?" then I congratulate your privilege.

I have two questions for you, reader: Are you free? And what would you do for the freedom to be anyone? Unless your answer is *anything,* try again.

NANCY

1988: FOUR YEARS OLD

In the early morning, in my footie pajamas, I cracked open the door to my mother's bedroom. I couldn't see anything except the orangey-red tip of her cigarette levitating over her bed as she took long, dramatic pulls in the pitch-blackness of the Connecticut morning. I often visited her before sunrise, as I never really slept and she frequently awoke in the night to smoke cigarettes in complete and utter darkness, the cigarette's ember seemingly the only light in the whole universe.

I silently shuffled into the room and climbed up her four-poster bed, which was so high it required a small staircase to scale it. Exhaling a whole atmosphere of smoke, she whispered, "My Sweet Baby James," as I wriggled my way under her layers upon layers of plush blankets and down comforters. I nestled my head onto her lap and she absently drew her long, bright-red nails over my back until I fell asleep, all the while puffing away consecutively on long Benson & Hedges cigarettes and blinking silently into the pensive darkness.

I loved these mornings, when I could snuggle with my mother and believe that she was always going to be my savior. That she alone, in a world that wouldn't let me rest, would be the one to lull me to peaceful, innocent sleep. That she would always be the fire-breathing dragon who had raised a little human boy named James.

CHAPTER 1

In 1948, a Sephardi Jewish man and a British woman had an affair in Spain that resulted in a secret daughter. They decided it was best to put her up for adoption. The daughter was sent to live with a wealthy Protestant couple, Robert and Cora, at their estate in Greenwich, Connecticut, and Robert and Cora named her Nancy Elizabeth White. The family had a large house staff: gardeners, cooks, valets, and maids, the most notable of which was Yeti, a maid who became Nancy's confidante.

Cora was a raging alcoholic who was said to have attempted suicide in front of Nancy on two occasions. It was much like the game of Clue: Mrs. White, in the kitchen, with the knife. Yeti the maid had stopped her before she could cut her wrists right in front of her daughter. Cora would play the role of perfect fifties housewife to guests and strangers, and then drink herself into a depressed oblivion.

Thankfully Nancy had her brother, Bruce, who was also adopted, for support. They forged a lifelong bond, vowing to protect each other from Cora's wallops, emotional or otherwise. When things got really bad, Nancy fled to her neighbors, the Bradburys. She spent many of her childhood afternoons learning to cook American cuisine with Mrs. Bradbury. This is where her love of cooking began. It certainly wasn't from seeing her mother cook, what with all the chefs and maids and such. Wealth can breed ineptitude.

As a teenager in the beautiful, ostentatious town of Greenwich, Nancy blossomed into a vision of 1960s beauty. She had long black hair that hung down to her waist and a thin, petite frame, accessorized with a pair of enormous breasts. Her eyes shone a bright hazel green. She was the American Dream. She wore frilly blouses and kept her fingernails long and filed, with a scandalous red shellac highlighting her fine, delicate hands. When she listened to music she'd close her eyes, twisting and turning her graceful hands in the air and rocking her hips gently side to side. Her joy was so easy at this time that she smiled wide and laughed loud for every photo taken. Her large teeth gleamed in the suburban sunshine as she gossiped with her best friends—the Boss Chicks, as they named themselves. They smoked cigarettes in profusion and freely passed around bottles of beer. They were the queens of the town, the envy of every American girl, and the lust of every 1960s American boy.

One summer, Nancy and the Boss Chicks met a group of older gentlemen at a bar. Among them was one Patrick Gil—"Pat," everyone called him. He was a tall, rakish man seven years Nancy's senior. He was happy and quick to laugh, with joyful almond eyes. Nancy and Pat began seeing each other regularly, going on civilized, mid-twentieth-century dates. They fell in love listening to Bob Dylan records on a portable record player in her family's driveway. Fresh, innocent romance.

Nancy's parents, the Whites, were not pleased with this new union. Pat's father was a Portuguese housepainter and his mother had once been the nanny to George Bush Sr. But Nancy had a way of making people see things her way. She was always the boss. She was smart, wily, unstoppable. She used her vulnerability to connect with people and draw them to her side. And she was undeniably *cool,* the very definition of charismatic.

When she discovered she was pregnant, she knew she might be pushing her freedom. She was eighteen and unwed, and it was the 1960s. So she and Patrick were wed immediately, and she gave birth to her first of five children, Peter. The happy couple built a house from the ground up on Hillcrest Lane in Old Greenwich. It was the envy of the town and as chic as they come. Patrick began law school, while Nancy stayed home. They were young, beautiful, and rich: on track to becoming the *perfect* American family.

For years, Nancy and Patrick were invincible. They decided to open a bar in Port Chester, New York, as the drinking age was eighteen there and twenty-one in Connecticut, and they wanted a place to party with all their friends. They named the bar the Stumble Inn, and it became the good-time place. Every rich teenager from Greenwich brought their parents' cash to the bar and danced and drank themselves into a stupor to the tunes of the Doors and the Rolling Stones. Nancy and Patrick were making money hand over fist and reveling in their good fortune. They had two more children, Melissa and Robert, rounding out their perfect nuclear family. Nancy was a child mother navigating the elusive maze of growing up. Like Cora before her, she played the part of the consummate Greenwich housewife: white Christmases, crystalline dinners, precious Easters, and polished silver.

1989: FIVE YEARS OLD

One of my favorite gifts that my mother bought me was a small watercolor painting of a little boy and his teddy bear. She said it looked just like her Sweet Baby James. Like the boy in the painting, I, too, had a teddy bear, which I had named Magic Bear. He was cream colored with a fat white tummy and an upturned nose, and I loved him as much as I loved any of my siblings.

On the watercolor painting, beautiful calligraphic writing spelled out, "Follow your dreams, for they hold endless possibilities." My mother took me by the shoulders and shook me gently, with a wistful gleam in her eye. "You listen to me, Jimbo. This. This is what it's all about," she said, tapping her painted finger on the word "dreams," which I could not yet read. She went on, almost ruefully, "Follow your dreams, for they hold endless possibilities." And she hugged me close, resting her chin atop my tawny head.

CHAPTER 2

In 1980, Nancy gave birth to another baby boy, whom she and Pat named Andrew. It had been eight years since Robbie, the next-youngest child, had been born, and this was obviously an accidental pregnancy. They had even talked about abortion.

Shortly after Andrew's birth, Nancy lost both her parents to alcoholism and cancer. Cora and Robert left her with a whopping $500,000 in a trust fund that was managed by Robert's brother, Warren White. In her trust fund was a significant number of shares in an oil stock called Occidental Petroleum, where Nancy's grandfather had worked. He had bought shares and created trust funds for his grandkids. Per her grandparents' and parents' wishes, Nancy would receive $150,000 per year, making her a millionaire by the mid-1980s. Pete, Nancy's eldest child, recalls her tearing open the mail voraciously, holding up the oil check, and kissing it with glistening eyes.

She and Pat bought a six-bedroom house of Gatsbyesque proportions located in the Shorelands gated community and situated on a private beach on the Long Island Sound. This incredible Manhattan satellite truly was the home of a millionaire and it reeked of old money.

That August, Nancy and Pat returned to the family's country club to show off their adorable baby boy. Every upstanding family in Greenwich was a member of the Innis Arden country club, home to a golf course and a swimming pool. The Gils hired the head swim coach and pool director, a twenty-two-year-old man named Stuart who had just graduated from college, to teach their children how to swim while they drank themselves silly and partied with their friends. Pete, Missy, and Robbie, as they were known, were real country club rats, getting into all sorts of mischief with their friends. They were independent little hooligans with a penchant for tricks and fun.

Stuart was the up-and-comer, the local hero, the all-star. He held every swimming record imaginable at Greenwich High and was the All-American heartthrob that only the 1980s could produce. Six foot three, with luminous blue eyes, a heroic nose, a trim, russet beard, and a broad-shouldered swimmer's build, Stuart was the embodiment of that era's prime macho energy. A feted jock, with wit to boot.

Nancy and Stuart saw each other every day at the pool. Soon, they began to find ways to spend more and more time together. The hometown hero and Greenwich's number one housewife were walking a thin line. Whispers followed Stuart wherever he went. "She's so much older." "Isn't he the kids' swim coach?" "He just got back from college." "She just had another baby with Pat and lives at Shorelands." "She's throwing away her life." But Nancy and Stuart didn't care, not one bit. They fell in love like only the forbidden can.

Nancy and Stuart would go on drinking benders together, disappearing into the weekend and leaving little Andrew with the nanny. When Nancy would return, completely inebriated, she'd knock on Missy's door and want to chat. Nancy confessed the whole affair with Stuart to Missy one evening. Missy, who was ten, started locking her door at night. Nancy was on a quick path to becoming her mother, an alcoholic.

The summer turned to fall, and the fall turned to winter. Pat could ignore the affair no longer. There was too much talk among the high society. He confronted Nancy and said calmly, "It stops now. I'll let it all go if it stops now, then we can move on."

She cried, "Let's go to counseling. Let's talk about it. Please."

"No. It stops now."

"But I love him."

She was head over heels. There was fire, passion, and intrigue. She couldn't stay away. Even in asking for counseling, she was prolonging the inevitable. The whole town was ablaze with the news. To this day, the older residents of Greenwich speak of the Nancy scandal, calling it "the local news of the decade."

1989: FIVE YEARS OLD

My mother often locked me in my bedroom for hours upon hours. I was not allowed to come out until I had taken a nap. But I never slept, not even at night. I was a nocturnal little child insomniac. "Where's the fun in sleeping? Can I color while I'm asleep? Can I play with my Ninja Turtles? No? Then why would I go to sleep?"

My mother would say, "You're tired. Little boys need rest. Go to bed or I'll sell you to the gypsies." And then she'd lock me in my room. I would lie down on the floor, press my lips into the crack under the door, and scream at the top of my lungs, an eardrum-rupturing din indeed.

I got so fed up with being locked in my bedroom that I once grabbed the Pac-Man-branded wastebasket, pulled down my pants, and pooped in it. "That'll show her!" I thought. But all it did was leave me trapped in a small room with a waste bin of human poop for the foreseeable future.

Another time, I opened the window, climbed out, and shinnied up two stories along the gutter. My brother Robbie spotted me from the pool deck and raced up the stairs to my room. He reached out the window and calmly told me he'd give me ice cream if I would come back inside. Clearly, it was the only thing I could do.

One day, I was locked in my room, but I couldn't find Magic Bear, who was my best friend. I looked everywhere. I ran, crazed, shouting for him. He never responded or showed his little upturned snout around a corner. I sat on my little bed and cried and cried. Had he left? Was I alone? I felt a despair that made every cell in my body tingle and vibrate. Torrents of tears flowed down my plump, asymmetrical cheeks. My mouth pulled down at the corners in a wailing frown.

Wiping my eyes, I looked out the window of my bedroom, only to be greeted by a cheerful blue sky. A sky that had no right being so beautiful when I was feeling so sad. "I bet he's out there," I thought between sobs. "I just know it. He needs my help." So I stood up on my bed, closed my eyes, and began to levitate a few inches off my L.L.Bean bedspread. I floated over to the window, undid the latch—which I had become very good at undoing—and zipped out into the cozy blue sky.

I flew at such a speed! I flew past the park by our house and found myself over my elementary school. My schoolmates were all there and enjoying recess on the playground. Principal Walsh stood stoically at the edge of the schoolyard, and as I flew by, I reached into my pockets and threw little pebbles at his shining bald head, laughing hysterically as I flashed to and fro.

I then found myself floating into the park, only to discover an enormous triceratops hot on my trail. I launched myself up and perched on the highest branch of the tallest, leafiest tree in the park. The triceratops was coming directly for me. "But I thought they only ate plants!" I shrieked aloud, hoping someone would hear me and be duly impressed by my encyclopedic knowledge of dinosaurs. The triceratops rammed its tricorne head into the base of the tree, but I had jumped off just in time. I hovered above the tree as countless boughs rained down on the dinosaur, who happily crunched and munched the fallen foliage. Smug, I said to myself, "He just wanted the leaves," and rocketed up into the troposphere.

I could feel Magic Bear's presence. I knew he was up in the sky. I looked in every direction and was greeted by adorable, fluffy white clouds. They looked just like cartoon clouds. I bounded to countless pillowy fluffs, searching for Magic Bear in vain until, on the highest, most remote cloud, I spied a log cabin. Great plumes of ashy smoke rose from the chimney and were whisked away by the breeze. I shot up higher and higher until I finally arrived at the log cabin in the clouds.

I walked up to the front door and knocked, but there was no answer. I trepidatiously turned the doorknob and entered. "Hello?" No answer. "Is anyone home? I'm James. I've lost my best friend. My Magic Bear." No answer. I looked around and was greeted by warm colors and cozy decor. It smelled of a happy hearth and fresh air, but there was no one home. I traipsed through each snug room until I found a child's bedroom, much like my own. I walked in, sat on the edge of the bed, and put my head in my hands. "I'll never find Magic Bear," I said aloud. As my eyes welled up with the tears of a woebegone child, I felt a tickle at my feet on the floor. Terrified, I snatched my little feet up onto the bedspread. "Monster!!!" I screamed. But then, silence. Trembling, I rolled onto my tummy and steeled myself, gathering all the courage I had displayed in terrorizing Principal Walsh and facing the not-so-carnivorous triceratops. "I can do this," I told myself. Propping myself up with my hands on the side of the mattress, I slowly and steadily lowered my face past the ledge. "OK, I'm going to look on the count of three ... two ..."

I awoke from my nap with a violent start. I was sweating lightly and a cool wind licked at my face from the open window, blowing the gauzy white curtains into the room. My eyes drifted from window to wall and fixed on the small watercolor painting. "Follow your dreams, for they hold endless possibilities."

I hopped down onto the floor and looked under my bed. There was Magic Bear, face down, smooshed on his cute little snout, with one eye peering out at me as if to say, "Took you long enough!" I reached in, rescued him, and gave him a hug as big as the world had ever seen and might ever see again. Happily, I thought to myself, "Some hugs you have to earn."

Mother was right. I was going to follow my dreams. I would learn to fly for *real*.

CHAPTER 3

The real drama began when Stuart's parents discovered the truth about his and Nancy's affair. His mother, Rose Mary Maunsell, was an austere, stern Englishwoman, not to be crossed. She had come of age in London during the World War II blitzkrieg. On her way to volunteer at the local hospitals, which is what young ladies were meant to do at that time, she walked past smoldering ruins. After completing two years of college, which was quite revolutionary for a woman in the 1940s, she decided to board a ship for the United States—New York City, of course. She was ready to escape the horrors of World War II London and seek adventure in America. Upon disembarking, she found a tiny apartment and applied for a job as an office secretary to earn some pocket money. There, she met George Walter Whiteside Jr., a kind divorcé twenty years her senior. He wooed and wooed her, but to no avail. Rose Mary was staunch in her solitude.

Weeks turned to months. George finally wore Rose Mary down, and the stoic Englishwoman and the genteel American fell in love. They married, settled in Greenwich, Connecticut, and had five children, including Stuart. George and Rose Mary thought of their family as English nobles settled in America. They were proper, haughty, and wealthy, but not terribly social. George's father was the American lawyer for Winston Churchill, for Pete's sake! So upon discovering that their youngest, star-athlete son was fraternizing with a married woman, Rose Mary nearly fell off her high horse. She kicked Stuart out of the house so swiftly he barely had time to gather a set of clothes. That was how an Englishwoman traumatized by World War II handled a tough situation in 1980: sweep it under the rug, or else chuck the whole damn rug out the window. George and Rose Mary shipped Stuart off to Dallas, Texas, to work for Exxon selling typewriters, effectively ending the affair between Stuart and Nancy . . . or so they thought.

But Stuart and Nancy never lost touch and never fell out of love. For a full year, Stuart went from house to house, selling obsolete writing instruments, while Nancy languished in her housewifery. She fell into a depression, which she treated with Klonopin and booze. She received countless love letters in the mail, ironically handwritten on Exxon letterhead by the typewriter salesman to whom she'd relinquished her heart.

EXXON OFFICE SYSTEMS COMPANY
12000 FORD ROAD—SUITE 200—DALLAS, TEXAS 75234

Nancy my love,

I love you. I miss you. I need you. I oftentimes wonder why we do it all. It seems so hypocritical to suffer all this pain just to feel happiness. Whatever, I will love you always. I need to be with you, no matter how much we must sacrifice.

I'm on the road now, making calls to people who don't want to buy, mainly because they don't need it. Eventually, I'll be able to convince them that they need it even if they don't.

Soon, we get a new product line and new prices. They are going to change the typewriter a bit and completely change the word processor. That will be good. Right now, the word processor is a real dog. All of the other systems I've seen can run circles around it.

Enough. I love you. Please take care of yourself. Keep the children happy for me. Hugs and kisses, etc.

Always,
Stuart

Stuart returned from Texas after understandably failing to sell a product that nobody wanted. He and Nancy began seeing each other again, much to the dismay of the entire town. People often mistook Stuart for thirteen-year-old Pete's older brother because he was so young. Nancy and Pat's children were humiliated by all the attention. Pete asked her one day, "Why is the swim coach sleeping in a car on the street?" Stuart was not allowed home with his parents and not allowed into the Shorelands house—Pat would've killed him—so he lived in his blue Toyota station wagon.

As winter enveloped Greenwich in a blanket of fresh snow, Pete confronted Pat and Nancy about what he had to finally accept: Nancy and Stuart were having an affair. In response, they told him they were getting a divorce. He replied, "Does that mean we're not spending Christmas together?"

1992: EIGHT YEARS OLD

Mortal Kombat for the Sega Genesis had just been released and I needed it. Video games had become a way for me to feel smart and capable. I was bad at baseball, bad at soccer, bad at football, bad at school—bad at everything except drawing, it seemed. I liked how video games had original art and music. I liked the puzzles and the coordination required. I liked that I could play them with my brother Andrew, who was so much cooler than me.

I was in my dad's row house in Bridgeport, Connecticut, talking on the phone with my mother. My dad had been living there ever since he'd started dating Katie, whom he had married in 1990. "It's not THAT violent!" I whined into the receiver.

"Absolutely not. I've seen it on the news. It's absolute carnage! You're eight!" she told me.

I went on to plead and beg for nearly twenty minutes. I told her that there was an option to remove the blood graphics and that playing video games did not mean I would become a murderer. "It's not REAL!" I shrieked.

I was very aware of my father and stepmother in the adjacent kitchen. They were speaking softly to one another and setting the table for dinner. When I got off the phone, my father said to me, "I'd never let you speak to me that way. You were begging like a dog."

I cast my eyes down in shame, knowing he was right. How could I forget myself in front of him like that? I felt sick. I hated myself. I sat down quietly, placed my napkin on my lap, and kept my eyes lowered so they couldn't see the tears threatening to spill over my cheeks.

That very same night, one town over, my mom went out with Andrew to Toys "R" Us and purchased *Mortal Kombat* so they could surprise me when I returned.

CHAPTER 4

In 1981, divorce was still fairly taboo. Nancy was forced to sell the Shorelands estate to shed her life with Pat and start afresh with Stuart. They decided they needed to get the hell out of Greenwich, where everyone knew their names and sordid story. Fairfield, another suburb of New York City that was slightly farther north on the Long Island Sound, seemed like the perfect escape. They bought—well, Nancy bought—a house on a street called Pilgrim Lane and moved the whole family, with Pat and Nancy's children splitting time between Fairfield and Greenwich.

It was a confusing time for all of Nancy and Pat's children. Missy and Robbie were certain that Nancy and Pat were getting divorced after nearly seventeen years of marriage solely because their neighbors, the Joneses, were getting divorced. Pete was distraught and filled with teenage rage at having to relocate, abandoning his high school and his friends. Andrew was a toddler and didn't know who his father was. Was it Pat or Stuart?

Stuart and Nancy were married in 1983. They were happy hippies, she in a boatneck, bell-sleeved, embroidered wedding gown and a flower crown, and he in a classic black tuxedo. He even shaved for the wedding. They were astonishingly happy. The way they looked at each other on their wedding day could make the sourest, dourest faces blossom into wide, toothy grins.

They took the kids in a newly purchased van on long camping trips, during which they'd booze themselves silly and smoke consecutive packs of cigarettes. Stuart taught the kids how to fish, to pitch a proper tent, to build a fire and grill hot dogs. He was young, sporty, and competent in a woodsy, classically masculine way—a tough stepfather not to like.

But he was twenty-five and had been shouldered with the responsibility of helping to raise four kids. There was no learning curve. It was a hard slam into fatherhood. Nancy helped him start his own carpentry business, which he ran out of a dusty red van. He struggled to make ends meet, and Nancy struggled with the reality of the failing business venture. He and Nancy drank to cope with their financial decline. She was consistently taking Valium, Fiorinal, Vicodin, Trazodone, Gabapentin, Klonopin, and other prescription drugs, nearly all downers. Booze was the glue that held them together.

1989: FIVE YEARS OLD

Pop, which is what I called him, used to take me with him to his carpentry jobs. I'd sit up in the rafters with him as he installed insulation or built out an attic. He'd hand me a two-by-four, a hammer, and a handful of nails to keep me busy. I'd sit next to the battery radio blasting rock and roll hits from the seventies and bang nails into the board while he drilled, sawed, scraped, and caulked.

We went on daily runs to "the dump" to deposit large pieces of wood and detritus, the refuse from the day's work. I loved to watch the enormous maw of the compactor chomp down on wood, metal, and glass. Rapt, I'd watch as entire wardrobes were reduced to shards of wood and metal.

One day, I didn't want to leave the dump. I refused to climb back into the van. Frustrated, he drove away without me, leaving me stunned next to the lip of the compacting pit. I was all alone, a five-year-old at the construction dump. I didn't know what to do. So I stood there and wept inconsolably. Moments later, Pop's red van returned. He swerved into the lot and jumped out of the driver's side. Scooping me up and squeezing me close, he said over and over, "I'm sorry. I'm so sorry."

CHAPTER 5

Shortly after Stuart and Nancy married, she became pregnant. She already had four children but was excited to have a child with Stuart. Despite her pregnancy she continued drinking excessively, smoking excessively, and taking prescription drugs.

Borrowing against her trust fund, she bought a large house on Colonial Drive, also in Fairfield. So inconsequential were Stuart's opinions and desires to her that she didn't even tell him she was going to buy it. That was how Nancy lived her life. Everything was and *should* be available to her.

The house would've made the Brady Bunch jealous. Stuart, in all his Davy Crockett–ness, beautified it with an incredible tree house nestled into an enormous oak tree in the backyard. He built a pool for the kids to swim in as well.

On July 27, 1984, James Bruce Whiteside was born at St. Vincent's Medical Center in Bridgeport. Stuart's parents wouldn't come meet their new grandson. They thought the affair turned marriage disgraceful. This was a great source of misery for Stuart. He was proud of the life he had created with Nancy and he wanted to share it with them, to show them it had all been worth it. James wouldn't meet his grandparents until two years later, when Stuart's father was dying of throat cancer and expressed a last wish to see his grandson.

With an infant in arms, Nancy decided it was time to get sober, and shortly thereafter, Stuart followed suit. They went to Alcoholics Anonymous meetings, fighting the beastly disease of alcoholism together. By 1986, they were both proudly sober, but with their sobriety came a price: they fell out of love.

Without the haze of drunkenness, Nancy became astoundingly aware of the lifestyle downgrade she had accepted to fulfill her desire to be with Stuart. She had left the comforts of being the Greenwich country club housewife to be the sole provider for five children and a husband in his twenties. She had funded a failing carpentry business and borrowed against her trust fund to impulsively purchase a large home. She became resentful of Stuart. She still wanted to be the Greenwich housewife she so clearly wasn't anymore. When James was two years old, she and Stuart filed for what turned out to be a very hostile divorce.

1988: FOUR YEARS OLD

My siblings were always watching PG-13- and R-rated movies. My mother would tell them, "You can't watch that," but then disappear into her bedroom. One night, Missy went to Blockbuster Video to rent a movie and came back with the comedy-horror film *Gremlins*. It was the most terrifying thing I had ever seen. I was beside myself with fear. I wouldn't sleep. I wouldn't be alone. I even thought a gremlin would pop out of the toilet and bite my butt. My imagination ran wild and I couldn't concentrate on anything. Around every corner lurked a gremlin to maim and dismember me.

My family grew exhausted from my fear. "Gremlins aren't real!" they'd tell me, giggling. I would cry and clutch their legs. "Please don't leave me!" I'd wail.

One night, I woke up screaming. I was sure there were gremlins lurking in each dark corner of my bedroom. My mother rushed into the room and scooped me up. "It's OK. Nothing's there. Gremlins aren't real. Don't be scared." I sobbed into her shoulder, shaking violently.

She stood abruptly and took my hand. "Come with me," she said, winking. "Let's sneak a snack." She and I used to wake up in the middle of the night, go to the kitchen, and make a bowl of Campbell's split pea soup. "Sneaking a snack" was our nocturnal rebellion and bonding time. We'd sit at the kitchen table and spoon the salty green mush into our mouths, whispering and laughing by the wan light of the stove.

"What are you so scared of?"

"They're gonna get me. I just know it."

"I know they seem real because you saw them in a movie, but gremlins don't exist. What you're feeling is fear. We've got to get rid of your fear."

"But how?"

"I know what we'll do. Come on. Up you get. Come with me."

My mother rummaged under the sink and extracted a brown paper lunch bag, then scooped me up and carried me into the family room, which was home to a large white-brick hearth. It was majestic and beautiful. Setting me down, she opened the fireplace screen, set a Duraflame log into the andiron, and lit the corners of the log with an extralong wooden match. Then she sat down on the sofa and patted the cushion next to her. I was confounded. It was three a.m. and here she was, lighting a fire! I climbed up onto the sofa and cuddled next to her.

"Fear is a nasty, nasty thing. It makes people do all sorts of craziness. It's much scarier than those gremlin puppets from the movies. You see this paper bag?"

"Uh-huh. Why?"

"Well, I want you to talk about your fear into this paper bag. Then we'll seal it up quick and throw it into the fire! Then, no more fear!"

"What should I say?"

"I can't tell you that. You have to be able to say it yourself, otherwise it won't burn up."

"Hmm. OK."

She opened the bag and held it out to me. I sat there for a moment, steeling myself, while the Duraflame crackled and spat in the hearth, casting shadows over the night-owl mother and son.

"I'm afraid of the gremlins. I don't want them to eat me. I know they're not real, but I'm still scared!"

"OK, now shout into the bag, 'I'm not afraid!'"

"I'M NOT AFRAID!"

She snapped up the bag and folded the top over. Yanking me off the sofa by my hand and dragging me over to the fire, she threw the paper bag into the happy blue flames, then began jumping up and down and laughing. "You did it! You did it!" I giggled and jumped up and down and spun in circles with a huge fire-lit grin on my four-year-old face.

She sat me on her lap in front of the fire that was joyfully consuming the paper bag filled with my fears and said, "You mustn't be afraid to speak your fears while I'm here to hear them. You can always talk to me, Jimbo."

CHAPTER 6

The Colonial Drive house was the epitome of late-eighties joy and excess. Thanks to the Occidental Petroleum checks, Nancy and the children could enjoy a wealthy, carefree life, buying anything and everything they wanted. Pranks and antics happened all over the place. The kids ordered Domino's pizzas and hid under the wooden steps to the front door. When the delivery man arrived, they poked kitchen knives up through the gaps in the wood, shouting that the house was haunted. They threw little James off the roof into the swimming pool. Robbie gave Andrew "swirlies" in the toilet by dunking his head into the water and flushing. Pete made yogurt-and-mayonnaise smoothies and told his siblings they were milkshakes. Andrew gave pieces of dry cat feces to James, telling him they were candy bars. They gathered acorns and climbed onto the roof to throw them at passing cars. They rode a twin mattress down the long staircase. They threw pillows down onto the first floor and dove into them from the balcony. Danger, mischief, mayhem, and independence.

Nancy was much like Peter Pan. She didn't want to grow up and she really *believed* the fantasy. Missy's friends loved to come over and smoke cigarettes in the kitchen with Nancy, gossiping about their lives and the boys they were dating. She was the coolest, funniest mom they'd ever met. There was always music playing and the music was always about freedom. Robbie took up the guitar and played constantly. He learned "Puff, the Magic Dragon" to play for James, whom they all called "Jimbo." The house thrived on creativity, and art was appreciated but never mandatory. It was the most human way to love art . . . for the very *need* of it. Nancy taught the kids that they could be anything they dreamed, all they had to do was try—which, for a wealthy white family in the eighties, was disturbingly accurate.

There were lavish Easters and generous Christmases in which the enormous tree was dwarfed by a sea of gifts. There was laughter and silliness. There were teenage parties and deception. Missy would often call the house when she was out with her friends and say, "I'm up in the playroom. Goodnight!" Nancy, being far too absorbed to take the steps, never made the trek to corroborate Missy's story. Other times, Nancy would call the playroom telephone line from her bedroom to ask Robbie to make her a sandwich. Little did she know he was having a party up there. He'd arrive with a ham-and-cheese sandwich and she'd casually remark, "You smell like booze. Behave. Thanks for the sammie." Then he'd return to his party.

Meanwhile, Stuart had met a lovely widow named Katie at Alcoholics Anonymous, hung up his carpenter's tool belt, and gone back to school to get a teaching degree. He began substitute teaching and then

landed a position as a high school English teacher in Stratford, Connecticut, where he continued to work for decades. He and Katie married and had two children together, George and John. Stuart and
Katie would later divorce after more than twenty years of marriage. It
seemed divorce was the new American dream.

1989: FIVE YEARS OLD

It was settled in divorce court that I would split my time between my
parents. Mondays with my mother. Tuesdays with my father. Every other
Wednesday with my mother. Every Thursday with my mother. Every
other Friday and Saturday with my father. And every Sunday with my
mother. I was shuttled around like a lost parcel.

In the beginning, my father had nowhere to live. On his custody days,
I'd sleep on the floor of his friend Chris's apartment. When my father met
and started dating Katie, we moved into her row house in Bridgeport,
where she had lived with her late husband, whom she'd lost to swift and
brutal cancer. I recall a photo of a dark, extremely handsome man with a
short, black beard. I often thought him the black-haired version of my roan
father, an alter ego perhaps. The concept of death eluded me, but I watched
her look at the photo with bright tears in her pretty, youthful eyes. It taught
me that every adult has a story no one can imagine.

My twin lives were confusing. At my mother's enormous house, I was
surrounded by my four siblings. Even though they were technically half
siblings, I loved them like we had been born of the same parents. My
mother gave us anything and everything we wanted. We had multiple tele-
visions throughout the house, a Nintendo Entertainment System, and a
swimming pool. Trips to the grocery store were like winning the lottery.
We'd slam items into the cart haphazardly: potato chips, ice creams, candies, sugar cereals, and snacks of every type imaginable. Upon exiting the
store, Robbie would place a head of lettuce atop my head and we'd yank my
T-shirt up over my face. He held my hand as we walked through the

parking lot garnering strange looks and scandalized scoffs from other families. We called this stunt "Lettuce Head." At the dinner table, my brothers would sometimes ask me to do "Lizard Boy," a character I'd invented that was half lizard, half boy. I'd morph my face into a Grinchly smirk and dart my tongue out of my mouth while hissing and manipulating a single brow. Another dinner stunt involved a character I'd made up called "Licky the Dog," in which I'd crawl around under the enormous dining table eating scraps out of my siblings' hands while they howled with laughter.

While my life at my mother's was bombastic, life with Pop was monastic. At Katie's row house, I missed my siblings. We ate steamed or boiled vegetarian meals and had no television. Every night, Pop instructed me to wash up for bed, something that just didn't happen at my mother's. As a child, I viewed him as terrifying and strict compared with my mother. I was an imaginative, silly child, but felt compelled to be a proper young gentleman around my father. His logic was intimidating. He was a father who made you feel stupid by simply existing.

He read to me every night. We'd sit in my tiny bed with the Sesame Street comforter and read Greek and Roman mythology, Jules Verne, Robert Louis Stevenson, Daniel Defoe, or my absolute favorite, Garfield. We used to laugh till we cried each time Garfield mailed Nermal to Abu Dhabi. These were the times I liked my father best—when we were giggling about a fat orange cat and learning about the mysteries of the world.

After reading, he would turn off the light and I would lie there silently for hours, afraid to get up and move around. The city of Bridgeport was quite violent in the late eighties, and I frequently fell asleep to the sound of rogue gunshots. Pop would fetch me from my bed and install me on a child-size inflatable pool float on the floor, next to his and Katie's bed. He kept a gun in a lockbox in the attic and a baseball bat under his side of the bed. Bridgeport was known as the murder capital of Connecticut. Cars were stolen, houses were robbed, and people were murdered. It wasn't news; it just was.

No matter what my father did, no matter how many right moves he made, he didn't stand a chance against my mother. I was switching back and forth between a Chuck E. Cheese and a convent. Naturally, I preferred pizza and Skee-Ball over quiet asceticism. For a five-year-old, there was no contest.

CHAPTER 7

One day in 1991, Nancy received a letter in the mail from Uncle Warren, who oversaw her trust fund. "No. No, this can't be happening," she said, despairingly. The Occidental Petroleum stocks had tanked, and her income, already greatly reduced as a result of her consistent borrowing from her principal, would be cut in half. There was no way she would be able to afford her current lifestyle and support her children on these payments. Thankfully, Pete, Missy, and Robbie had already gone away to college, leaving Andrew and James the only kids at home. But all the same, Nancy was hemorrhaging money, and she needed to change her lifestyle drastically if she was to avoid bankruptcy.

Years earlier, she and Stuart had bought an investment home on Reef Road in Fairfield, a shack they rented out to college students. They called it the Barnacle Party House, and Pete's girlfriend had been one of its tenants. It was actually a shack, infested with flies and rodents, with stucco walls and seven-foot-high ceilings.

Nancy sold the Colonial Drive house, evicted the college students from Reef Road, and moved in with Andrew and James. It was a dumpy downgrade. Nancy, the Greenwich debutante, now lived in a shack with her sons by different fathers. When Pat dropped Andrew off at the new house, he sat in the driveway with his head in his hands and wept. Andrew asked, "Why are you crying?"

"It's a shack. She lives in a shack," Pat whispered, mostly to himself.

But Nancy was a resilient woman. She got a job selling perfume at the local department store, aptly named the Fairfield Store, where Missy had worked years prior.

During this time, Nancy still lived a life of excess, even if the house was shabby. There were only brand-name foods to be found in the pantry, nice clothes in the closets, and plenty of pocket change to go around. She knew it wouldn't last long, though. Uncle Warren was no longer allowing her to borrow from the principal of her trust. She had already nearly depleted it. Selling perfume would not give her the life she had been accustomed to, so she decided to begin nursing school. She had an ability to make people comfortable that lent itself perfectly to being a nurse.

She was a brilliant student. She'd sit on her bed with her books strewn about her, taking copious notes late into the night and often forgetting to eat. She loved learning. Her beautiful handwriting covered countless Five Star college-ruled notebooks.

Nancy still wasn't drinking, but she was smoking like a chimney and taking various prescription pills, which had been prescribed by the very doctor who'd helped get her sober from alcohol. Whether from stress, alcoholism, or pills, she developed two ulcers on the lining of her intestine. She'd wake up in the middle of the night and stagger to the miniature bathroom, where she'd sit on the closed toilet, doubled over in agony. Andrew and James would wake to the sounds of her moaning. Finally she had the ulcers surgically removed, but the surgery caused her to develop "dumping syndrome," in which the contents of the stomach empty too quickly into the small intestine, leading to frequent nausea and dizziness.

In 1992, a powerful hurricane flooded Fairfield. The waters of the ocean rose and rose, spilling into the town. Nancy's home, which was just a stone's throw away from the beach, was filled nearly to the ceiling with salty seawater. Pete and Robbie, along with the fire department, used a small dinghy to paddle to the house to rescue the dog and the cat.

They wept as they waded through the shoulder-high water, dodging Andrew's baseball cards and Nancy's school notes, which were soggy and floating on the surface. They found Gus, their golden retriever, and Chloé, their calico cat, perched atop the kitchen counter. Gus and Chloé were best friends, even though they were different species. Gus stood on all fours with his head above the water, and Chloé cowered atop Gus's shoulder blades, shaking violently from the cold.

The whole house was muddy and waterlogged. Dead fish and long strands of seaweed covered the furniture and beds. The walls were stained with salt and grime. The patio furniture was found floating in the park a few blocks away. Nancy didn't have home insurance, and this came as a severe financial blow to a woman who was already doing everything she could to ensure her financial stability.

It was all too much. The divorces, the devaluation of the oil stocks, the moves, nursing school, the ulcers, the flood. Nancy wept at her misfortune, from the guest room of Pete's fiancée's apartment, where the whole family had gathered for shelter. Heidi, Pete's fiancée, was in awe of the White/Gil/Whiteside family. They sat together and laughed and told jokes. She thought about this life-defining tragedy— the loss of one's home—and then looked at the family, who were at that moment hugging and singing along to the *Aladdin* soundtrack together. Heidi smiled ear to ear and chuckled at the beauty of this strange group of individuals: Pete the pragmatist, Missy the boss, Robbie the jokester musician, Andrew the sweetheart, and James, the silly and gentle youngest son. She thought to herself that Nancy was a brave warrior.

She went to the guest room and knocked lightly on the door. "Nancy? It's Heidi. Can I come in?" Cracking the door, she saw Nancy sitting on the edge of the bed, holding in one hand a long cigarette, its ashy end long with spent tobacco. Her other arm was folded under her cigarette-arm elbow, and her legs were crossed as she pensively gazed off into space with red, bleary eyes.

"Jesus H. Christ. What the hell am I going to do?"

"Nancy, just come with me. I want you to see this. Just be quiet."

Heidi led Nancy out of the guest room to the hallway, where she stopped and told her to look around the corner into the kitchen. Nancy's five children were sitting at the kitchen table, drinking Nestlé's Quik and laughing hysterically as Robbie reenacted the genie's lines from *Aladdin*. James was sitting on his lap and singing along to the music. They were boisterous and full of energy, despite the day's events.

"They're so beautiful, Nancy," Heidi said.

Nancy laughed quietly and then began sobbing. Heidi pulled her into a hug, and they stayed there like that for quite some time.

1988: FOUR YEARS OLD

The first word I learned how to write was mom. I was so proud of my achievement. I always fancied myself a genius, even though I was held back in preschool and had horrible grades during my time as a student.

I thought, "I'm going to show her what I've learned!" I went into my mother's bedroom and rummaged through her vanity, which was home to multitudinous perfumes, phials filled with bright tinctures, powders, poufs, shadows, lacquers, and lipsticks. I filched a bright-red lipstick in a shiny silver tube and sped off to the den to carry out my task. The den was home to an enormous beige sectional sofa. It was a custom piece of furniture that must have cost a fortune. There was also a behemoth of an ottoman, which I climbed onto. Unscrewing the Lolita-red lipstick, I scrawled the word MOM in enormous letters across the entire surface of the ottoman.

As I was finishing my final, careful stroke, my mother walked in, froze, and screamed at the top of her lungs. "James Bruce! NO!" She snatched me up and the lipstick fell from my hand as she carried me like a football into the large kitchen. I knew exactly where she was going and what she was about to do, but I didn't know why. Why wasn't she proud of my achievement?

She plunked me facedown on the counter, whipped my trousers down, reached over to the utensil crock, fished out a large wooden spoon, and began whacking away at my behind ragefully. I cried and screamed, but she didn't stop. I didn't know why I was getting the ever-threatened wooden spoon.

Truth is, my siblings and I got the wooden spoon rather often. Our mother was constantly whooping one of us. Perhaps it was barbaric, but you'd better believe I never wrote on any furniture ever again. I don't condone that sort of abuse, although I don't feel knowingly damaged by it. But it's the wounds you can't see that do the most damage.

Conversely, Pop beat me only once. He had promised me that we would go to the zoo one Saturday and that there would be wolves there. We had piled into the car for the early Saturday AA meeting when it started pouring rain. Pop and Katie looked at each other meaningfully, but I didn't register their telepathic communication. As usual, I sat on the floor during the meeting, eating the alcoholics' Oreos and coloring in my books.

When the meeting concluded and the folding chairs were put away, my father steeled himself and told me we weren't going to the zoo that day; it was far too rainy to be enjoyable. I lost it. I had a nuclear meltdown. I screamed and kicked all the way back to our Bridgeport row house.

When we arrived, they sat me down at the kitchen table and tried to reason with me through my noisy paroxysm. Unfortunately, emotion hears no reason. Fed up, Pop dragged me up the stairs and spanked me into next Tuesday. It was the only time he ever hit me.

After all these years, I remember nothing but the shame of having had such an emotional outburst. I'd forgotten myself. The pain of a spanking was nothing compared with the loathing I felt for myself. Bury the emotions. Bury to protect.

CHAPTER 8

With the help of friends and family, the flooded Barnacle Party House was cleaned and de-molded, and the family moved back in. Nancy would bend but she wouldn't break. She graduated from nursing school in 1994 with the great distinction of magna cum laude. She was forty-six years old. She had raised five children and been divorced twice. No more would she downgrade herself to support a man.

Nancy found work as a nurse immediately. She worked at two hospitals and various nursing homes before she settled on a private practice, Dr. Donald Gorsuch's office in Fairfield. She was a wonderful nurse and the patients and staff adored her. She made them feel comfortable and heard, so they weren't afraid to be vulnerable with her. On one occasion, Dr. Gorsuch even confessed to her that he was having an affair with one of the other nurses. She had that effect on people. She could draw out anything, even one's deepest secrets. The patients would ask for her by name: "Is Nurse Nancy in today?"

Nancy had a boyfriend for a while, a fellow nurse named Bob. He was a parody of a bachelor, with dyed black hair and a clean-shaven face. He drove a sky-blue 1967 Chevy Impala convertible and owned an absurd home with a twisting indoor koi pond running through its many rooms. Nancy often took Andrew and James to this silly home while she spent time with Bob. She'd give them snacks and plop them down in front of the television. At the time, James had braces and a palate expander, a metal device that affixed to the roof of the mouth and molars for the purpose of barbarically widening his upper jaw.

One day, while James was watching TV at Bob's and eating a coffee yogurt, which he loved, his palate expander popped open and essentially exploded. Half the metal device lodged in the back of his throat. He spluttered and coughed and cried. Andrew ran to get Nancy and Bob. They took a look inside his mouth and saw shards of metal sticking into his uvula and esophagus. They called an ambulance but there wasn't time to wait. Bob reluctantly sat James up on his kitchen counter and forcibly cut the palate expander out of his mouth with a heavy pair of wire cutters while tears carved canyons into James's flushed cheeks. Nancy and Bob split up shortly thereafter. Bob the bachelor was not yet ready to be Bob the stepfather, though Nancy had hoped he would be.

One of Dr. Gorsuch's patients was a gruff man named Paul and he was an alcoholic. He came to the office to be prescribed a drug called Antabuse, which is said to treat alcoholism by creating a nasty reaction to alcohol: nausea, dizziness, rapid heartbeat, and chest pain. His nurse was none other than the lovely and charismatic Nancy White, no longer a Gil or a Whiteside. They began dating immediately.

Paul was a thin man of medium build with a Rat Pack appeal. His heavy brow sat on top of large blue eyes and a straight, noble nose. He worked as a display coordinator for Home Depot stores across Connecticut and smelled of freshly sawed wood and heated metals. He smoked Marlboro Reds, loved music, and had a sullen, blue-collar mien. He thought Andrew and James were hilarious and befriended them immediately. With the help of Antabuse, Nancy, and counseling, Paul got sober, and he and Nancy were engaged and married within a year.

Nancy, Paul, Andrew, and James moved into Paul's rental home in a different part of Fairfield. Nancy, having joined the workforce, pooled her money with Paul to demolish and rebuild the Barnacle Party House into a lovely beach house on stilts that would protect it from the frequently rising tides. But during construction, Nancy was diagnosed with toxic shock syndrome, a life-threatening complication of certain types of bacterial infections. Nancy didn't know exactly how she'd gotten it, but her symptoms were severe. She had a high fever for an extended period and her skin developed bright, angry rashes. Her eyes and throat swelled and reddened. Her hair fell out in patches.

Thanks to Prednisone, a steroid, Nancy conquered the toxic shock syndrome as the last shingles were being put on the new house. The illness had taken many weeks of work and pay away from her, but she was happy to be in her new home with her new husband and her youngest children. She went back to her job at Dr. Gorsuch's practice. She felt like she was finally making it all work. She was healthy and she had a good job and a home she was proud of. She loved decorating the home in a beachy theme. There were pale blues and greens and large prints of seaside vistas. With all the windows open, you could smell the salty tide drifting on a cool breeze.

1999: FIFTEEN YEARS OLD

Dance had eclipsed everything. I knew I would become a professional. There was no question. I had decided it and therefore it would be, so strong was my delusion and determination.

My mother had remarried. I genuinely liked Paul. He laughed at my jokes and secretly gave me five-dollar bills so I could go to 7-Eleven to get a hot dog and a Slurpee. When we moved back into the newly renovated Reef Road house, Paul gave me a stereo receiver, a five-CD player, and a two-tape deck with two speakers for Christmas. I was overjoyed. It was one of the best gifts I'd ever received. For a teenager, music is often the only way to feel seen and heard.

I was going through a lot. I was struggling with my sexuality and mired in denial. I was doing poorly in school, which I couldn't care less about, and I had invented a deep and powerful loathing for my father and his strict, structured, austere household. Nancy spent a lot of effort to negatively influence my view of Pop. She'd spit out vehement diatribes about his shortcomings, calling him all sorts of horrible things. As a naive child, I'd never thought to question them.

Everything confused me. The growing distance between me and my closest brother, Andrew: the two young boys who had played Sonic the

Hedgehog with Doritos-stained fingers were long gone. The taunts and jeers of my schoolmates, who didn't understand my alien mannerisms and speech. The continuous rebellion I felt against my schoolteachers, all of whom I thought were inept and determined to demonize me. The devastating effect of a stillborn child on my stepmother and my father. The blooming relationships with and care from my dance teachers, who felt like a surrogate family. My burgeoning sexuality and experiences, which I didn't ever want to talk about or confront. And finally, my gravely ill mother, relegated to her sickbed with a mysterious illness.

My mother let me take innumerable sick days. She knew school was tough for me. She saw the way it made me feel. I never talked about it. I never wanted to talk about anything, but she knew. She always said that she could feel everything I felt, that she had ESP. Andrew was always furious to find out she had let me stay home. "He gets to stay home all the time!" he'd shout at her.

Sometimes, I think she just let me stay home so she could hang out with me. She and I would gather snacks and watch marathons of Star Wars. Every time, she'd say, "You know, people say I look like Princess Leia. Don't you think she's pretty?" And I'd say, "Of course, Ma."

On one of our "mental health days" she sat me down and taught me how to do a tarot reading. She loved mysterious spirituality and found higher meaning in everything. She'd draw the cards gravely, theatrically. She taught me cat's cradle and how to knit. And she and I made countless meals together. Our mental health days were fun and full of laughter and silliness. She tried so hard to teach me spirituality and empathy, but I just couldn't get it. I didn't get it.

CHAPTER 9

Nancy was enjoying her life until she developed another high fever. Her toxic shock had returned, and this time, it was even worse. She remained in her bed for a very long time. Nurses came by to administer intravenous drips and dole out painkillers. All her hair fell out and her skin bubbled and blistered. She turned a livid pink as her skin burned off from the inside out. Her finger pads shed their prints and became white, scarred, senseless things. Her eyebrows and eyelashes fell out as her lids swelled and turned purple. The steroid Prednisone was again prescribed. Her face and body swelled and bloated. Her fevers raged. Here was Nancy, who had just turned fifty, put herself though nursing school, endured a home-wrecking flood, rebuilt a home, and married a lovely gentleman, and now she was bedridden with a mysterious, painful, debilitating illness. Her whole body burned. She was a fire of pain, fury, and disappointment.

This second toxic shock syndrome was the hole into which she fell, like Alice in Wonderland. Nancy suffered a classic opioid addiction before it was headline news, leaning heavily into the painkillers and downers she had been dabbling with for her whole life: Valium, Fiorinal, Vicodin, OxyContin, Trazodone, Gabapentin, Klonopin. The grit and power she had displayed for the last fifty years was beginning to wane. "How can I keep fighting?" she thought. "All I do is fight. I'm so tired." Her body was draining her ability and willingness to fight. She lay in bed, hooked to an IV, groaning in pain as she swelled and swelled, her skin flaking and burning off. With tears in her crusting, turgid eyes, she asked someone, anyone: "Why?"

1999: FIFTEEN YEARS OLD

When my mother was diagnosed with the second bout of toxic shock syndrome, I was deep into my teenage angst and shame. I took her a big glass of Coke, with extra ice, as she always instructed, and set it on her bedside table. An IV and vitals machine beeped and dripped beside her. She looked at me and said, "Jimbo. You never visit me. Do you even care if I die?" I didn't know what to do or say, so I just rolled my eyes and retreated to my room. She had a flair for drama and was trying to manipulate me into professing my deep need for her and her love, but I didn't know how to do that. It was unnatural to me.

The truth is, I didn't really care. I was so selfish and I didn't understand how sick she was. I could barely bring myself to look at her. She was horrifying, with her skin all burnt off. At fifteen, I couldn't identify fear. When I look back, I see now, I was so scared. Good God, was I scared. But my fear prevented my feeling anything. I stuffed it down and away, God forbid I cry or display any sort of emotion. I hated crying. I wouldn't do it. So I went to high school and I went to my dance classes. I went to parties and I won dance competitions. I learned how to drive and I ignored my father. I went on and moved on and kept myself busy until I didn't care about my dying mother, for fear I might actually feel something.

CHAPTER 10

It took time, but Nancy recovered. Her hair grew back and her skin healed over. Andrew went off to college and James came out of the closet as a homosexual. There were grandchildren and happy birthdays. Life barreled on.

As a result of her illness, Nancy had missed out on so much work that she and Paul were forced to sell the Reef Road house and move to Milford, Connecticut. They bought a simple house close to the home of Pete, Nancy's eldest. Nancy began a part-time job as a night nurse at Fairfield University, where she saw many an alcohol-poisoned student.

Fresh out of toxic shock hell, she was utterly dependent on prescription pills. She took so many, they gave her a slightly loopy gait. On her drive home one night, she crashed her car and shattered her femur. It is not known whether she was overly medicated. She simply drove her car into a telephone pole. A surgery was performed on her leg that made her nearly bionic. Plates and screws littered her bones, which had been made brittle by the Prednisone. Yet again, she was relegated to her bed.

Paul kept working and took care of Nancy as she convalesced. He was a good caretaker, with a patient bedside manner. He made sure Nancy was comfortable as she got used to using crutches. He made sure she had her beloved large Dunkin' Donuts order, which the employees called the "Crazy Nance": an iced latte with extra ice, two pumps of vanilla, and whipped cream. He brought her packs of Marlboro Light 100s, which she had switched to a few years earlier. They were enormously long cigarettes. Truth was, she'd light a cigarette, forget about it, and move to another room. There might have been at least three cigarettes burning in any room at a given time.

Paul stood valiantly by as his new wife suffered pitfall after pitfall. But he was a man with demons of his own. When Nancy, doped up on her pills, lost her balance and fell, re-shattering her already bionic femur, it was the straw that broke the camel's femur. He took the car out and came back with a bottle of cheap vodka. He twisted off the top and took a swig. Sweet, sweet coping mechanism. Paul had lost the battle with alcoholism once again.

Nancy became despondent and understandably depressed. She was incredulous at her misfortune, which seemed comical in its frequency. Upon finding out that Paul had begun drinking again, she blew a gasket. Their marriage devolved into trivial squabbles and gibes. They dug into each other with sharp, abusive words. The love and care they had built their early marriage on evaporated, replaced by injury, pettiness, and deceit.

As Nancy's health improved, so did her resolve to leave Paul. Andrew had gone to college, and James had left for ballet boarding school in Virginia. They had no distractions from their ire. One dark evening, Nancy called the police on Paul. She claimed that he was neglecting her, that her injury had left her disabled and he was leaving her in her upstairs bedroom for days at a time. When the police arrived, she kicked him out of the house, shouting, "Get out! Just don't you dare take the Klonopin!"

2001: SEVENTEEN YEARS OLD

When I returned to Milford, Connecticut, from Virginia School of the Arts for Christmas, I was greeted by a filthy house. My mother was still healing from her second broken leg and she had recently kicked Paul out. I didn't know where he had gone, and I didn't ask. I was so disappointed in my mother. Who the hell was she? What was happening? This would be her third divorce. I didn't want to judge, but of course I did.

I really liked Paul. I loved him. He was a dream of a stepfather. He accepted me immediately when I came out, even though my mother had gone through a strange journey of her own regarding my homosexuality. He'd cook me tasty goulash when I returned from a late-night dance rehearsal. He never judged me the way I felt everyone else did. He saw who I was and thought, "Sure, why not?" He was also depressive and was constantly being tested by the realities of being alive.

I looked at my mother, in her full leg brace, and realized how small she was. She wore pajama shorts that exposed the horseshoe-shaped scars on both knees from her days as a gymnast. Her exquisite hands were marred by toxic shock. Her once perfectly painted nails were now a jumbled mess of lacquer, with color blotched haphazardly over her cuticles, and her bottle-bleached hair was thinning. I didn't understand the feeling I felt. Many people just watch their parents age. I was watching my mother disappear.

We spent a lot of time together that Christmas. I was home for a full week and I asked her to start teaching me all her recipes. She was a wonderful, unhealthy cook, which meant everything was delicious. We went overboard that week. She taught me how to make her famous chili, her orange-glazed ham, her pot roast, her meatloaf, her corn soufflé, her chicken pot pie, her chicken à la king, and Grandma Jennings's hot fudge. She wasn't terribly mobile, so I was getting a real hands-on crash course in the culinary arts. I watched her revert to the Greenwich housewife she used to be as she directed me to dice, pour, sift, grate, and simmer. I must've asked her to start teaching me her recipes because I had realized she was mortal. A mother is forever until you're faced with the reality that she isn't—that no one is.

She stood with a Marlboro Light 100 dangling from her poorly lined lips while she sang along to Joni Mitchell's "Cactus Tree" blaring on the small Bose CD player. She had introduced me to so much music. Once, when I was very little, she handed me a Walkman cassette player and headphones. I went to the room I shared with Andrew, hopped onto the top bunk, and pressed play. It was Christmastime, and "The First Noel" began to play through the tinny headphones. I sat on my bunk, clutching my blue-and-white knit blanky, and cried inconsolably. Andrew was confused and fetched our mother to come into the bedroom. He asked her, "Why is Jimbo crying?" She looked up at me on the top bunk and said, "Sometimes, something beautiful makes you cry . . . and that's all right."

While I busied over the stove, mixing up her famous chili, she removed her cigarette, looked at me, and asked, "Am I still pretty?" And I said, "Of course you are, Ma." But the question just made me sad.

CHAPTER 11

Nancy was on disability pay and her trust fund payments from Uncle Warren were, at this point, next to nothing. She lived alone at the house in Milford until her funds were depleted. Pete, who had begun a family of his own with Heidi and lived in Milford's charming seaside neighborhood called Woodmont, bought a condominium for Nancy, just a few blocks from his home. She would downsize to a two-bedroom apartment and pay rent to him. Pete and Missy also started managing

Nancy's paperwork and bills. They found her to be in dire financial straits. Nancy spoke constantly of Uncle Warren. She'd say, "We just have to wait for Uncle Warren to pass." She was waiting for an inheritance.

Nancy spent nearly all her time at home in her apartment, smoking cigarettes, drinking coffee with hazelnut creamer, and ordering things from QVC, a TV channel geared to at-home shoppers. Nancy was famous for giving gifts. She had the most generous soul imaginable. She loved providing for people and feeling needed. All throughout their childhood, her kids had lived a life of excess. Nancy even bought a secondhand '88 Chrysler LeBaron convertible for James when he got his driver's license. It was $1,000. The retractable top was broken, and he had to hold the wheel halfway turned to go straight, but it was a great, sporty vehicle.

Nancy's nuclear family always gathered every year for Christmas, even though her children were scattered across the United States, living exciting, dramatic lives of their own. For Christmas in 2004, Nancy went a bit overboard. Her mobility was limited by her leg and the residual weakness from having toxic shock twice in a row, so she did all her shopping on QVC, buying multiples of everything: bedazzled pens, gemstone keychains, ornaments, blouses, purses, tool kits, baubles, books, scarves, blankets, kitchen utensils. When Missy came over to pick her up and take her to Pete's on Christmas Day, she was stunned by the Jenga stacks of cardboard boxes completely filling Nancy's small living room. Nancy instructed her to load the boxes into the car. Missy did as she was told. That Christmas, each child and niece and nephew opened strange, unnecessary gifts with bewilderment and confused faces.

After that QVC Christmas, Pete and Missy staged an intervention. They asked Reverend Jim, a local clergyman, to attend and show his support. In doing her paperwork, Pete and Missy had found $7,000 in overdraft charges to her checking account and nearly fifty revolving payment plans on her QVC account. Nancy, who was of course smoking a Marlboro Light 100 and drinking extra-light hazelnut coffee, acknowledged that she was "maybe overdoing it a bit" and vowed to cut back. Robbie called QVC and placed her account on a "do not buy" list that prevented her from ordering any more items.

The children were then stunned to learn that Nancy had purchased a dog from a local breeder—a sheltie, which is a miniature collie breed. She named her Sunny. Why a woman in debt would purchase an expensive purebred puppy was beyond their comprehension. Sunny was a happy, beautiful dog, with smart, friendly eyes and a gentle demeanor. Though Nancy shouldn't have bought her, Sunny was the best thing to happen to her in a long time. They became best friends. Nancy loved sitting in her blue recliner, smoking cigs into next week, watching Anderson Cooper on CNN with Sunny's head in her lap.

2000: SIXTEEN YEARS OLD

I had been shuttled back and forth between my parents' houses since I was a toddler. Being a teenager and coming to grips with the reality of one's court-ordered custody is an unpleasant affair. When I was a wee bonny bairn, I'd simply scream bloody murder as my father dragged me out of my mother's front door. "Just let him stay!" she'd plead. "He doesn't want to go with you!"

"This is the arrangement."

At sixteen, I was ready to emancipate myself from my dry existence at my father's house. He and Katie had moved with their two sons into a pleasant home on Catherine Terrace in Fairfield. I had spent much of my time finding ways to never be at his house. I have rehearsals. I'm staying at a friend's. I'll be away for a dance competition. I conspired with my mother to confront my father and liberate myself from the clutches of my settled-in-court custody. I wanted to stay at my mother's at all times.

Mom and I sat him down in the living room of the Reef Road house, the house that they had bought together, and that she had knocked down and rebuilt with another man. I picked at my cuticles as I quietly told my father that I didn't want to live with him anymore. He replied coolly, "OK. I understand."

I think I know now what he meant. He saw the bond I'd forged with my mother over the years that had shaped me into her minion. As I said before, he didn't stand a chance.

CHAPTER 12

Nancy was becoming more and more fragile. Her skin was damaged and thin from toxic shock, and she consistently bruised and cut herself simply from grazing a wall or the edge of a chair. She was diagnosed with an iron deficiency and began receiving intravenous immuno-globulin infusions that bolstered her compromised immune system. These infusions made her weak, and it became clear that leaving her alone at her condo with Sunny was not safe.

Pete and Missy arranged for her to be moved to a two-bedroom apartment in an assisted independent-living community in Shelton, Connecticut. There were nurses on staff who would frequently check on Nancy and administer her medication and infusions. Once again, her life was downgraded. She crammed as much of the furniture from her previous lives into the tiny apartment as she could. Thankfully, Sunny was permitted to stay with her.

When Andrew returned from college and his new life on the West Coast, he sat on the street and wept for her, as his father, Pat, had done more than a decade earlier. Watching this exquisite, brilliant, vibrant creature languishing caused him real pain.

These years were scary for the family. The addiction and denial played out in a sick loop. Nancy's childhood friend, inexplicably nicknamed "the Wolf," successfully convinced her that she wasn't really an alcoholic, and they sat together often, drinking bottles of wine that the Wolf brought over. Nancy's children anguished over her lapse in sobriety. They watched as Nancy dismantled herself, taking chip after chip from them in a game of emotional poker. They became closer than ever, bonding over the savagery of being adults.

After one of her wine-soaked evenings with the Wolf, Nancy took Sunny outside to the large field behind the apartments. She was standing there, pulling at a cigarette, when she lost her balance and teetered over the edge of the single step into the field. Her shoulder shattered as she hit the cold, hard grass. She passed out from the pain and was not discovered until the early morning, when Sunny's shrill barks alerted the groundskeeper that one of the tenants was in danger. Nancy was patched up, given more pain medication, and sent on her merry way.

Once again relegated to her apartment, she dove back into the comfort of material purchases. One of the perks of being married and divorced three times is a wealth of aliases to choose from. She signed up for QVC from her new address, this time with her maiden name, Nancy White. This name and address had not yet been added to the "do not buy" list. When Missy inspected the bills in her mail, she discovered the new QVC charges, including $14,000 in recurring overdraft and interest charges. During one visit to Nancy's, Missy witnessed forty boxes arrive in the mail from QVC.

Uncle Warren passed away in 2010, leaving Nancy the remainder of her inheritance. Her trust fund had been whittled down to $40,000—by no means a small number, but nowhere remotely resembling the millions of dollars she'd once had. Uncle Warren also left her and her brother, Bruce, a simple house in Old Greenwich. They were both struggling financially, so they sold it immediately. With the help of Pete and Missy, Nancy began paying back the multitude of debts she had amassed over the last decade. She liquidated assets willy-nilly, pawning her three engagement rings and family heirloom jewelry without telling anyone. Lacking in funds but rich in experience, Nancy began to look toward the future.

2008: TWENTY-FOUR YEARS OLD

Every year, after Christmas at my brother Pete's house with the rest of my mom's side of the family, my father picked me up and drove me back to my life in Boston. The drive took anywhere from three to five hours. I believe this was a stroke of genius on my father's part. He knew that if he was given the time, he'd crack me. I'd sit in the passenger seat of his white sedan, fidgeting and biting my fingernails while he asked me questions. We'd speak about books we were reading, real estate, and investments. The fear of saying something stupid made my words sound boxy and rigid.

I remember him saying once, "You know, when you said you'd become a professional dancer, I thought to myself, 'Sure, whatever.' But you've actually done it!" I knew that was his way of saying, "Holy shit, am I proud of you!"

I began to see Pop in a new light. He became a person instead of the idea of the person I (and my mother) had invented. He spoke to me honestly about his battle with alcoholism and how he didn't go a day in his life without wanting to light a cigarette. He also said that turning back to alcohol would completely destroy his life. I admired his strength. He confided in me that he would divorce my stepmother when my younger brothers were off at college. I began to question why I had forever feared his judgment. What about a father is so intimidating? Why does it take so long to realize that everyone's the same shade of shit?

I had long figured out that the math surrounding my mother and father's marriage and my birth didn't add up. I had once asked my mother, "Were you and my father together before you divorced Pat?" Naturally, she vehemently denied it. I relate to her very much in this way. Protecting the idea of her was worlds more important than the truth. But on one of these rides back to Boston with my father, I asked, "Did you have an affair with my mother? She denied it, but I don't think I believe her."

You should have heard his laughter! A great big roar of mirth. He dabbed his eyes and said, "Yes. We had a very dramatic and scandalous affair. I was your siblings' swim coach and . . . well . . . there you have it."

CHAPTER 13

In 2015, Nancy went to see the doctor who performed her immuno-globulin infusions. A routine visit turned into the discovery of lung cancer, which evolved into liver cancer. She began radiation treatments immediately. The chemotherapy made her violently ill. Her hair fell out and she became weak. She hated every moment of this fight. She'd call her children and say, "I'm so tired. I'm just so tired. Do you know how long I've been fighting?" And she wasn't just talking about the cancer.

The doctors bought her time, but it was a terminal diagnosis. James called his father, Stuart, to tell him the news. Stuart then called Nancy and asked if she wanted to talk. She obliged and he drove up to Shelton and they sat and talked for three hours. Stuart's clothes reeked of smoke so badly afterward that he just threw them out. He began driving Nancy to doctor's appointments and even drove her sometimes into New York City, where James was now living and working. He'd text James to say, "Your mom is so funny."

2015: THIRTY-ONE YEARS OLD

After my mother was diagnosed with terminal cancer, she wanted to come see me dance one last time. Missy and Heidi arranged to take her into New York City to see me dance the lead in a new ballet called *AfterEffect*, by Marcelo Gomes. During this ballet I am visited by a spectral, motherly being, played by Misty Copeland. She descends from the heavens into my arms. She does not touch the floor until halfway through the pas de deux. She strokes my hair and comforts me as I writhe in anguish to a swelling Tchaikovsky score. I thought of my mother in the audience, dying of cancer and high on painkillers, and cried into my hands as Misty was carried away from me, into a bright white light. It all felt too on-the-nose to affect me so, but then again, sometimes on-the-nose is just how you feel.

After the performance, my mother came backstage with Missy and Heidi. She was dwarfed by her winter coat and her bare head was covered by a turquoise scarf. Her makeup was layered on heavily, and her too-bright dentures gleamed an impossible white. She could barely speak, she was so heavily medicated. As I danced, I had imagined her effusively rushing backstage, gushing over my performance, and telling me how proud she was. The reality was slow, dull, and gray. She stood, eyes sparkling and unfocused, and wheezed, "Jimbo." My sister and sister-in-law fed her questions as though she were a child. "Wasn't it beautiful? Aren't you proud? Wow! Weren't the lights lovely?" We posed for a photo together for the sole purpose of having a photo of Mom's Last Ballet. I smiled widely, more of a grimace really, and felt too much and nothing all at once.

CHAPTER 14

After her diagnosis, Nancy was celebrated and feted. Songs were written for her and meals were made in her honor. She even received a fancy wig that she could wear if she chose. At one party, she donned the wig and began calling herself "Diva." She then went on to do a five-minute bit about the character she'd spontaneously invented as her children and grandchildren howled with laughter. She wore faux-fur coats and dressed up in her best clothes. She screamed along to Robbie's songs in proud exultation. She hoisted her leg up to the side, a cigarette dangling from her mouth, to show James that she was still flexible and he got his dancer's legs from her. She told Pete that he was making "Christmas Breakfast," a soggy 1950s-style soufflé, better every year. She laughed with Missy about all their private dramas. A mother and a daughter have an incomparable, complex, and beautiful relationship. They made the best of the time they knew would disappear far too soon.

2016: THIRTY-ONE YEARS OLD

Things were really beginning to pick up steam in my career. I had arrived in New York City as an unnecessary invader, but the ballet audiences were warming up to me and I was working like a dog to solidify my place in American Ballet Theatre's illustrious ranks. I was proud of my hustle and couldn't believe how much my work was paying off.

My mother had decided she could no longer endure the chemotherapy. She did her last session in the spring. She said she wanted to live a little before she died. To know when you're going to die must be a strange thing indeed. She was stoic and joyful as she faced death. I think she secretly thought to herself, "Finally."

My father had been helping my mother with various tasks over the last few months, mainly doctors' appointments. He happily kept her company as she prattled on about this and that. She asked him if he would take her into the city to see me and he obliged. They drove into the city on a Sunday and we had brunch together in my neighborhood, Murray Hill.

I had never seen my parents together until that day. I had seen them pass each other coldly, but I had never seen them truly communicate. When I was a child and they'd drop me at the other's house, they wouldn't even come to the door. There was a wall of thick, immobile ice between them. To find myself sitting at a circular table in Midtown Manhattan with my parents—my actual parents—rocked me. There were no siblings, no stepparents, no new dates, no nothing. I was the sole product of the two adults sitting before me and I had never seen them together.

Nancy was weak of body but sound of mind that day and laughed heartily as they reminisced about their rowdy times in Greenwich. We ate mediocre food and marveled at the Manhattan prices. It was so normal that it made me nauseated. I wanted so desperately to love sitting there with them, but really, I resented how easy it was for them. I wanted to shout, "WHERE THE FUCK WAS THIS MY WHOLE CHILDHOOD?!" But I smiled and sipped my coffee and ate my cold eggs. "That was nice," I said, as my father helped her into his car and they drove away up Third Avenue.

As American Ballet Theatre's spring season drew nearer, so did my mother's imminent death. I felt its presence looming over me in every rehearsal. The guilt I felt for being away from Connecticut and feeling as though I was neglecting my dying mother weighed heavily on every bit of my being. Pete and Missy always bore the brunt of Nancy's needs—logistical, financial, and emotional—while I donned sparkly outfits and fought for applause. I felt the frivolity of my work like never before, and at the same time reveled in it and its ability to shake me out of my self-pity. Art feels like complete nonsense until you realize how much you need it, how it gives you the tools to survive in this world.

I took the train from Grand Central to Bridgeport every Sunday to visit my gravely ill mother. One Sunday, my father picked me up at the station and drove me to my mother's apartment, where she was receiving hospice care. She was happy to be home instead of wilting in some stark hospital. He dropped me off and told me he'd be back in the late afternoon to pick me up. My older brothers and my sister came over to the apartment and we sat with my mother, who remarked that she didn't have her teeth in. She was loopy with medications and looked simultaneously happy and like she was crying. Robbie took out his guitar and sang a song he'd written for her called "Chin Up." She just bobbed her head. She couldn't understand the weight of the moment. Meanwhile, we five children were beside ourselves with emotion, dabbing our eyes with the most plush toilet paper imaginable. She refused to ever shy away from the most luxurious paper

FINALLY.

products, regardless of her financial standing. There's something to be said for that sort of dignity.

Robbie's song goes like this:

It's not your fault
It's not something you've done
I know that this doesn't happen to everyone
But rest assured
You're gonna be all right
Hold on tight
And keep on fighting till you see the light
So keep your chin up
Because I know that you've had enough for today
It's OK
It's OK

Another Sunday, my father picked me up from my bedside vigil with my mother. He walked into the back bedroom, where my mother was resting. I was sitting with her, listening to music and reading, when she cracked open her eyes. She took one look at Stuart and reverted to the Stuart-hating Nancy from previous decades. She hissed, "YOU! You asshole! You motherfucking asshole! Get out! Get out! GET OUT!!!!" Struggling against her guard-railed bed, she shouted and swung her emaciated arms in a show of strength that I hadn't seen in weeks.

Pop's face fell and his skin grew pale. I could hear the breath catching in his throat. He stood speechless for a moment while she swung at him futilely. The hospice nurse ran into the room and tried to calm her. Her eyes rolled in her head and her lids fluttered. I stood there watching this scene mute and frozen. The last time I had seen them together, she was laughing at his jokes and reminiscing about their time as Connecticut's number-one rule breakers. I saw the pain it caused my father, who staggered and muttered, "I'll go." He shuffled past me while she kept shouting, "Get out! YOU FUCKING ASSHOLE!"

I got into his car. We sat silently for a moment. He kept his eyes cast down and let out a terse breath.

CHAPTER 15

Toward the end, her body became thin beyond recognition and she lost all of her brittle teeth. The cancer had quite possibly invaded her brain. As she lay there dying from cancer of the lungs, she forgot that she ever smoked.

2016: THIRTY-ONE YEARS OLD

I got a message from Pete on the morning of June 29. He said, "It's time. Get over here." I was at the theater and getting ready for ballet class and a matinee performance of *The Sleeping Beauty*. I looked at my phone, looked at the time. I was already putting on my makeup. I texted, "What should I do? I've got a performance at two." And this is the perfect way to sum up my life choices. Any major life experience has been eclipsed by my duty to my art. Not even being summoned by the imminent death of my mother can make me miss a performance. What does that say about me? I looked at my phone and knew I would do the performance. I hated myself every moment of it, but I did it. I didn't tell anyone about what was going on, because it was easier to hide.

I took my bows for a mediocre performance. I smiled and gestured and collected the requisite rose from my ballerina. I shook hands with the conductor. I turned and smiled at the corps de ballet, who glanced at me with medium interest. The curtain came down and a gap was pulled open for front-of-curtain bows. I led the princess out in front of the majestic gold curtain of the Metropolitan Opera House and we took ceremonious, lengthy bows. The corners of my mouth parted to show my teeth in a strange, monstrous, crooked grin. "What the fuck is wrong with me?" I asked myself. I thought myself a sick person.

We disappeared behind the curtain and my boss and my coaches descended upon me with smiles and a general performance of support. As they approached, I turned to my partner and said, "I've got to go. Thank you," and I ran back to my dressing room in the Principal Hallway. I tore my costume off and scraped my makeup off, dry, with a towel. In a few short moments I was out the stage door and making my way to Grand Central Terminal.

I arrived at dusk. My mother lay semiconscious and unable to speak. She was hooked up to various machines that were clicking and beeping happily. Her nurse hovered over her with deep care in her eyes. Pete, Missy, Robbie, and Andrew were there. We hugged and I apologized for always being last. They laughed at my makeup-smeared face. I knelt next to her and whispered, "I'm here, Ma. I'm sorry I'm late. I love you."

She held on through the night. I slept at Pete's and we went over to my mother's apartment early in the morning. Her whole family was there with her. All five children, their spouses, her exes, her grandchildren. She was stable but slowing down. We sat outside, drinking coffee in the back field, in the cruel late-June sunshine. The nurse leaned out the back door. All she said was, "Come." We silently mobilized, just us five children, and rushed into our mother's bedroom.

My brilliant, complicated, unicorn of a mother lay in her sickbed, a mere wisp of her former glory. There was a dark, thick scent in the air. The beeping of her life-support devices mingled with the wheeze of her short breaths. Her peanut head sported the fuzz of a cancer patient who has forsaken treatment. Her mouth lay agape, toothless, and slightly skewed. Her arms were riddled with bruises and scabs. Her skin hung off her bones. That's what she was: skin spread unceremoniously over muscleless bones. Her hands, which had been a symbol of her grace and strength, were all spots, tendons, and flakes. But it was her eyes that took my breath away. She lay there with her eyes wide open and unblinking. Her beautiful hazel-green eyes were bloodshot and clouded over with a greenish-yellow slime. I looked at her supine body and felt my blood cells raging in mine. I felt the joy and the pain of our thirty-one years together. More than anything, I felt love.

We stood in a horseshoe around her bed and clasped hands, including hers, and formed a ring. We said, "Mom. We're all here. You can go now, if you want." Missy said, "No doubt you'll do whatever you want anyway." And we all laughed, though hot, fierce tears blazed in our eyes. Even here, faced with death, the children turned to laughter and love. Each of us in turn told her how much we loved her, and how much she had taught us. Life had been relentless for her. It took and took and took and yet she still managed to give us the only thing that truly matters. She gave us our souls. She gave us everything that made us special in a world of people hell-bent on being normal. She taught us to dream. More than that even, she gave us the gift of one another.

She took her last breath and we waited. Her breathing did not resume. We stood hand in hand and cried softly, respectfully. One by one, we filed out of the small bedroom. I was left alone in the room with her. I sat on the edge of the bed and looked around. A corkboard hung on the adjacent wall. I walked over and examined the many things pinned on it, one of which was a rectangular blue plastic name tag that read NANCY WHITE, R.N. I plucked it off the board and held it in my nail-bitten fingers. The pin represented so much about my mother. I thought, "This . . . is grit." I tucked the pin into my pocket and never told my siblings that I had taken it. I don't know why.

I went back to the still form of my mother and gently kissed her on the top of her head. I whispered, "Thank you, and I'm sorry."

HOW I MET JESUS
CHRIST ON GRINDR

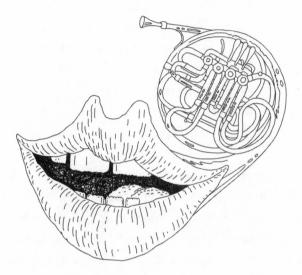

How did you start dancing?" This is the number-one question that strangers ask me.

I always want to ask them in return, "How did you start bleaching your anus?" or "How did you start curling at the Olympic level?"

The truth of the matter is that my answer to that common question is rather commonplace, although I wish it were more exciting. Do you ever wish you could zhuzh up your life? What sort of tales would you spin? Maybe you would be a chihuahua breeder from Chattanooga named Chooch, or perhaps your mother would be the inventor of meth. In the spirit of the immortal wisdom of the Spice Girls in "Spice

Up Your Life," here are my many paths to dancing—including the real story.

MARTHA STEWART

"How did you start dancing?" the plastic surgeon asked.

"Well," I replied, "when I was nine years old, Martha Stewart's car broke down in front of my mother's house on Christmas Eve. It was raining cats and dogs out there and she used a *Hustler* magazine to shield her face from the rain as she skipped up to our front door. I saw her coming and opened the door and shouted, 'Come on in! It's better than prison!'

"We made ourselves extra-dirty martinis and had a sock hop, just the two of us, listening to the Temptations and the Supremes on vinyl. She had this one great move in which she'd spin as fast as she could, holding her full martini glass in her hand. She spun so fast that she was able to turn her glass completely sideways without spilling a drop of her martini. When Martha stopped, she said, 'Now *that's* centrifugal force.' To which I replied, in my prepubescent falsetto, 'No, Martha, that's centrifugal *fierce*.'

"She chortled and told me to give it a whirl. I kept tripping over my feet and spilling my booze. It was frustrating being a drunk nine-year-old who didn't know how to twirl. 'Just keep trying,' Martha advised me. 'When they put you in prison, just keep plotting a path forward—or in this case, around.' I tried and tried again. Each time, I spilled my martini and had to remake it, and in that way I perfected Martha's perfect dirty martini recipe. We got completely hammered. Finally, I heard Martha shout, 'You're doing it! KEEP YOUR PINKY LEVITATED!!!'

"We giggled together until the sun came up. She made me a spinach and feta frittata, took her *Hustler* off the counter, and whispered through a proud smirk, 'Keep twirlin', kid.' And that's how I started dancing."

NO SCRUBS

"How did you start dancing?" Katie Couric asked.

I cast my eyes downward and said, "I'm not sure you want to know. I was just a kid. Well, I was heating up a Hot Pocket in the microwave when suddenly there was a quick flash and a *pop!* I turned to the television, where Mariah Carey had been singing in one of her music videos. I could still see her, but now there was no sound. I hadn't muted it, had I? I flipped to another station. An episode of *Seinfeld* was just beginning, but there was no trace of the theme music. The episode continued and I could hear the dialogue, but the hilarious, bass-slapping theme music was gone . . . vanished! Panicked, I ran to my room and turned on Z100, New York's number-one hit music radio station. The DJs were saying, 'Next up, Guns N' Roses' 'Sweet Child O' Mine.' And then there was complete silence, which lasted for about three minutes.

"That's when I realized what had happened. I had been transported by my pepperoni Hot Pocket into a dimension without music! I paced the room saying, 'Think, James. Think!' I opened my mouth and tried to sing the song I knew best, Madonna's 'Like a Virgin,' but there was no sound. I ran back to the living room, to the television, where TLC's 'No Scrubs' music video was now playing. I watched their mouths move, but I heard silence. I closed my eyes, tried to imagine the beat, and began to rock from foot to foot.

"'What was that?!' I whispered. I had heard something when I moved from one foot to the other. So I tried again, this time adding a bit more oomph to my moves. Huzzah! I could hear a bit more of the music!

"By this point, I had realized that the harder I danced, the more music I could hear. The only thing for me to do was to dance as though no one was watching. Nobody was, anyway. I leaped and twirled from love seat to sofa, from sofa to ottoman, from ottoman to basket of fuzzy blankets, completely losing myself in the swell of the almost-music. Tears burned in my eyes as TLC crescendoed, 'NO! I DON'T WANT NO SCRUB!' and *pop!* I was back in my own dimension by the time Left Eye finished her rap. The next sound that really was music to my ears was the *ding!* of the microwave: my Hot Pocket was done. And *that's* how I started dancing."

THE TRUTH: ELTON JOHN AND A PHONE BOOK

Bless my parents. They tried—separately, as they divorced when I was two years old—to find an activity that suited me. My father put me into Cub Scouts, which is the little-kid version of the Boy Scouts. I was a member of Troop 84 for a while, but I ultimately asked to quit because I found knot tying and charitable acts insufferable. We had a meeting once and the scout leader said there would be brownies at our next meeting. When the promised "brownies" were in fact little girls, it was the nail in the coffin for me. Very young Girl Scouts are called Brownies. WHAT ABSOLUTE FUCKERY!!! A decade or so later, my father would assist my two younger brothers to complete the program all the way up to Eagle Scout, which basically means you're the President of Earth.

My father also tried to get me to commune with nature. He took me on fishing and camping trips. I liked camping because I got to eat hot dogs like they were real food and we roasted marshmallows on an open fire. Fishing, however, was tough for me. I do not like worms. I do not like their slimy bodies or the fact that they don't have faces. When my father asked me to place the bait worms on the hook, I shuddered in horror. And if we caught a fish, forget about it! I was not touching that prehistoric beast!

My father's efforts were valiant indeed, and relentless. After the Cub Scouts failure he enrolled me in a local Little League Baseball team. I was appointed the enviable left field position. My older brother Andrew was very good at baseball, but it was pure comedy how bad I was. I'd be out in left field doing cartwheels when a ball would come flying at me and land with a thud several feet away. I'd freeze, standing with my feet together, and look down at the ball with my head cocked at an angle, like a cat unsure whether to pounce. Our team was sponsored by the local Dairy Queen franchise and we were promised free ice cream cones if we won. But we never won. Not even once. We were so pathetic that at the end of our final game, our coach said, "Aw, hell. We're going to Dairy Queen," and he bought us all ice cream sundaes. That was easily the best part of my Little League experience. Horrible things are always made better by ice cream. Dairy Queen would play a large role in my future, in the drag queen posse the Dairy Queens. Ah, sweet homosexual revenge.

There were a few one-offs as well. I went to gymnastics class a few times, but I was ultimately too apathetic to return. I took about two piano lessons before I realized I wasn't the next Beethoven and asked to quit. I played the French horn, which is that hilarious tubular horn that one must fist to play. My teacher said I had great French horn lips, which is just disturbing. I joined a soccer team for about two practices before I decided it was too dangerous for my dainty, princess-like constitution. I found my youthful contemporaries to be complete brutes and I found most authority figures to be dummies. I was a sensitive young thespian! Where was *my* much-needed creative outlet?

I spent the summer of 1993, when I was nine years old, at my mother's house playing video games on our Sega Genesis, eating Cool Ranch Doritos, and drinking Crystal Pepsi. I had not yet discovered masturbation, so I actually had a lot of free time. I was sitting at the kitchen table, probably eating something horrifying, when there was a loud *whomp!* next to my plate. My mother had thrown me the phone book and shouted, "Find something to do. You're driving me nuts!"

I chuckled and began leafing through the phone book (which in pre-Internet days was home to the phone numbers of houses and local businesses), searching for an activity appropriate for a nine-year-old. There was a large, full-page ad for a local dance studio. It featured a photo of a man holding a woman up over his head with one hand. It looked more like an ad for a circus school than for a dance studio. My curiosity was piqued. I asked my mother, "What's this?" and she said, "That's the local dance school. Want to go?"

I said, "Yeah," and that was it. We drove to the studio, which at the time was called the Dance Fitness Connection. It was located in a very 1980s racquetball club, and the dance studios were clearly built for aerobic Jazzercise. "Step class" paraphernalia lined the walls, and there were bright, geometric paint splashes here and there.

Thinking back, there had always been flashes of dance in my life. My father had given me a plastic Fisher-Price record player when I was very young. He fancied himself quite the audiophile. I'd go down to the basement to browse his vast record collection, select a few, and bring them up to my room—after asking permission, of course. A favorite of mine was Elton John's *Goodbye Yellow Brick Road*. Before I even knew what dancing or choreography was, I could be found in my bedroom, choreographing dances to Elton John's music.

Each fall, the studio offered a week of free trial classes to attract new students. When my mother and I arrived, the receptionist told us a jazz class was about to begin, and I asked if I could take it. I wore my street clothes: a pair of shorts and a T-shirt. I didn't have jazz shoes, so I just wore my socks. The music was loud and reverberated off the racquet club's walls, Michael Jackson hee-hee-ing and hoo-ing at an earsplitting volume. We did isolations of the body and coordination exercises, and then moved across the floor in unison, spinning and jumping. The class finished with a routine.

I can't say I was immediately good at dancing, but I liked it anyway because I was having fun. The most fun I had ever had in my life! That first dance class was pure joy. The music. The energy. The movement! It was a ship in the distance, and I was a castaway starving on a lonely isle. Dance shouted, "Ahoy! There's someone on that lonely isle!" and I replied, "Please save me! Help!" And *that's* how I started dancing. For real.

BONUS CONTENT: JESUS

Jesus Christ of Nazareth and I met up at Boxers, an LGBTQ bar in Chelsea. We had met on Grindr earlier that week and his profile said "Visiting." I sent a photo of my torso and asked, "Visiting from where?" He sent back a photo of his face wearing a *beautiful* crown and said, "Nazareth, stud." I love a visitor. I feel like everybody in this god-damned town knows who I am, so it's nice when I can be anonymous for once. I told him that my name was Bot.

Jesus and I chatted for a while and then we exchanged photos of our penises. Upon mutual penis approval, we decided to meet for a drink at a local bar. I like Boxers because all the bartenders are straight, and they don't want to fuck me like everybody else does. The DJ was playing Ariana Grande's "God Is a Woman" and I heard Jesus mutter under his breath, "This lady doesn't know what she's talking about."

It was actually a really great date! He was really nice and had kind eyes. And what a beard!!! His body was totally ripped. I could see it through his tight ribbed tank, which had what looked like a large ketchup stain on the front, by his ribs. It was February, yet he still wore sandals . . . so masc. Butch guys don't feel the cold. It's been proven. Meanwhile I was dressed in my best furs, looking like a god-damned Muppet.

Once we got our drinks (red wine), he suggested we get some food. He got up and fetched us some bread, saying, "You hungry for my body?" I loved talking to him and I could tell he was really listening to me because he rested his calloused hand on my thigh. I asked him what made his hands so calloused and he responded intimately, whispering very close to my ear, "I work with wood." My body shivered. He told me all about his woodworking business, which he called Jesus H. Christ Carpentry. The company specializes in livestock troughs and mangers.

Jesus said, "Enough about my wood. What about you?"

I said, "I'm a ballet dancer."

Then he asked the loathsome question: "How did you start dancing?"

Ugh . . . Jesus Christ.

COMING OUT IN Y2K

Here Lies
James's
Heterosexuality

1984 - ca. 2000?

W hen I was young, I'd introduce myself as *Jame*, for fear that speaking the letter *s* would reveal my plausible gayness. It's bizarre to me that one's sexuality should decide the nature of one's social standing and be used as a tool to separate and subjugate. I am a cisgender gay man, but it took quite some time to get to that understanding. Many little boys have faced the fear of being gay and, more important, the fear of *seeming* gay.

As a kid, I was very silly and had a great imagination. I loved the Ninja Turtles and singing and video games. I idolized my brothers. I grew up in a big family in a great town, and with a lot of love. I knew I was different, but that had nothing to do with my sexuality. Being the youngest of my mother's five children, I often felt special. This feeling was unfounded, as my siblings are all quite brilliant. I have enjoyed the benefits of feeling special all my life, though. It's given me the delusional self-confidence I *thrive* on.

My feeling of "otherness," however, began to manifest in elementary school. I was a very popular child, with more playdates and girlfriends than you can imagine. I had lots of friends who were girls, so the adults labeled them my "girlfriends," foisting upon me, a child, an unknown sexuality, which to this day I find intolerable. I played hopscotch and double Dutch and was particularly ferocious on the jungle gym, doing backflips and somersaults that would make today's recess monitors have a coronary. I also liked that the girls were always smarter than the boys. I fancied myself smarter than the boys, too. It was very obvious to me that I was not like them.

My first dick encounter took place in the first grade, when I went to my friend Charles's house for my first sleepover. Charles's hair was white-blond and buzzed into a mohawk. We ate dinner with his very kind family and played games, after which his mother instructed us to go and put on our pajamas. When I turned around, Charles was completely naked, pulling his pud, and proclaiming with pride, "I HAVE A PENIS!"

Horrified, I shrieked and ran out of the room to find Charles's mother. "Mrs. Charles's mom, I'd like to be taken home. Will Jeeves please bring the stagecoach around?" Why did it startle me so?

During the following years, I began to notice boys in a way that I didn't notice girls. But I didn't think of myself as gay or even really know what being gay meant. One summer when I was eight or nine, my brother Andrew, who was four years my senior, invited his best friend to stay at our uncle's farm with us. Justin Giletti was a lanky Italian boy who was always very nice to me even though I was Andrew's annoying little brother. I was fascinated by Justin. I couldn't tell you what he was like, or what he liked to do, but I remember thinking he was wonderful. One morning I was lying on the carpet watching cartoons when Justin walked over to me, wearing nothing but a pair of baggy boxer shorts as he passed by. Herein was my second dick encounter. I gazed up the wide leg of his boxers and glimpsed his dangly sex, and felt something akin to awe. This unidentified preoccupation was completely new to me, and I didn't give it much thought. I thought being enthralled by Justin's penis was the same thing as obsessing over Cool Ranch Doritos . . . and maybe it is? I adore Doritos. To no avail, I spent much of the remaining days at the farm on the floor, hoping to catch another glimpse.

My FIRST DANCE SCHOOL in Fairfield was famous for having an abundance of male students, a rarity for dance schools. I started there when I was nine years old, and for the first time, I made friends who didn't judge me according to the rules of public school. Our niche interest overpowered our fear of one another. My two best friends were Kurt and Jordan. We were the Three Musketeers, and we did everything together. We were the same age and had many of the same interests: comic books, video games, and dancing. We even each had many girlfriends, often swapping them out for one another. There was no shortage of girls to date at a dance school, which is a common reason young boys say they dance. "I'm around girls in leotards all day. You're just around other guys! You're the gay one!" This is a line we've been fed by our dance teachers and family members for decades. God forbid the reason we dance isn't linked to our toxic masculinity. God forbid we just like fucking dancing to Janet Jackson.

Kurt and Jordan were both from affluent, model families. Their parents were still together, with Lexuses (Lexi?), convertibles, and huge houses with separate bedrooms and unused rooms. I spent almost every weekend at one of their houses. Perhaps that's why I'm so hell-bent on hustling in my adulthood.

When we were twelve, we discovered Skinemax, the late-night showings on the Cinemax channel, which Jordan had at his house. We'd play video games until about eleven p.m., then turn on Skinemax, hoping for a flash of side boob or a besocked cock. By this point, I was vaguely aware of my attraction to men, but I wasn't able to pinpoint it. It was a quiet instinct. The truth is, I didn't even understand what homosexuality was. It wasn't portrayed on TV as a real, viable existence. I viewed my attraction to guys as similar to a lust for murder or bank robbery. To this day, I have no interest in pulling a big heist or chopping up strangers to flavor a stew . . . I just like dudes.

Kurt didn't get the Cinemax channel, so when we stayed at his house in Newtown, we'd go to his playroom, turn on the TV, and flip to the Spice Channel. He didn't actually get that channel, either, so it was scrambled and every porno looked like an acid trip where you'd occasionally see someone getting pounded from behind, or a bounce of a breast on the lap of a friend. These sad attempts at watching porn often morphed into a scene in which we'd hide our bodies under a blanket and furiously masturbate. These scenes exhilarated me, as the nearness of other male bodies was something I didn't yet know I enjoyed and didn't really have a personal definition for. I attributed my eagerness to the hilariousness of the scrambled nineties porn and the feeling that we were really getting away with something good. I wonder if I watched the porn at all, or if I just stole surreptitious glances at my friends while feigning interest in Spice Channel wobble-morph boob.

One night at Jordan's, I went to brush my teeth and returned to the bedroom to find Kurt and Jordan completely naked and performing fellatio on one another—sixty-nine-ing, if you will. I froze, stock-still, in the doorway. "Wh-wha-what are you doing?"

"James, come join us," they replied in unison, as if they were asking me to join the communal (cummunal) table at a church potluck. "We've been doing this for a while and thought we should include you," Kurt added. Society had cultured me to want to scream "GOD

HATES FAGS!" and run to the nearest police station, but part of me said, "These are my best friends, and who cares?" I was backing away, horrified, when Jordan stood up and led me to the bed, where I had my first explicitly homosexual experience . . . a threesome.

I was very young, but reader, before you're horrified, I challenge you to speak openly about your history of sexuality with yourself. This was a free, beautiful environment to explore my sexuality. It wasn't about being gay or straight or whatever, it was about getting off with my best friends. In retrospect, we were in a quasi throuple before there was a name for it, for about four years. We did all the things parents would have nightmares about—sex, drugs, parties, orgies—but we did it all in a group of trusting, loving friends.

It wasn't all dicks, dicks, dicks. I had many experiences with girls as well. In fact, my biggest regret about this era is that I had girlfriends the whole time. I felt that if I had a girlfriend, I couldn't actually be a homosexual. I was with one of my girlfriends for almost two years, and she, like most of the other dance students, knew about the sexual history between Kurt, Jordan, and me. I'm mortified that I used her to make myself feel better, and I'm horrified that societal norms made a thirteen-year-old boy think he needed to con a young woman into dating him to hide his obvious homosexuality. These are wrongs that affect a life. These are wrongs that change people into almost-people.

I always kissed the girls, but I never kissed the boys. I thought that if I kissed them, I'd be gay. I could suck their dicks into next Tuesday, but if I kissed them, *then* I'd be gay. Jordan often tried to kiss me, which for some reason was egregious to me. I found his hot breath revolting, even though I was attracted to him. My mind had somehow convinced my body to be repulsed by intimacy. Despite all these sexual exploits, intimacy was something I had yet to discover. When I look back at my attempts with girls, they feel like self-imposed sexual molestation. Like my mind was hijacking my body to perform an unnatural and unwanted deed at the horrifying expense of these unwitting girls. These were extreme, sick acting exercises I implemented upon myself. "Can I be what I'm supposed to be?" I'd ask myself. "Can I play this part?"

AT SIXTEEN, I was essentially a horny E.T. with acne and bad grades. My friends knew I was gay, but I still vehemently denied it, even though I wore skin-tight Gap sweaters and knew every lyric to every *NSYNC song. JC was my favorite, and in my nightly wanks I'd frequently envision him and Ricky Martin getting it on.

Enter Noah, an out-and-proud, tall, blue-eyed brunette with straight teeth and a Hollywood jawline, who wore his hair in the ski-slope swoop popular in 1999. He was a geeky theater guy who just happened to be devastatingly handsome. He was a senior and his mature body fascinated me. I was introduced to Noah at the local coffee shop, which is naturally now a Starbucks, and I fell for him immediately, even though I was still closeted. We had friends in common and consistently ended up at the same parties.

One night, at a party at my friend Al's, I noticed Noah paying me more attention than usual. We were smoking blunts and drinking our requisite forties of Olde English when he said, "I'm feeling pretty tired. I'm gonna go upstairs for a bit." He headed up the stairs and I watched him go, feeling perplexed. Who gets tired at a teenage party? But then a force stronger than reason lifted me out of my seat. I placed my forty on the coffee table and floated across the burnt-sienna, medium-pile carpeting as Missy sang knowingly, "Hot boyz . . . Baby, you got what I want." I silently ascended the stairs, telling no one my destination, and slipped into the first-floor living room, where Noah lay supine on the sofa. The only illumination came from the stove light, which shone from the adjacent kitchen. Large green houseplants glinted in the weak glow and a dull, club-next-door din emanated from the floorboards.

I sat on the floor, perpendicular to Noah. Neither of us said a word. He dropped his right hand over the edge of the sofa and ran it through my hair. This was my first taste of sensuality. I was frozen in place as he single-handedly (literally) changed my mind about myself.

After what felt like eons, I turned to look at him. His left hand cradled his head like a pillow, and his right continued stroking my hair and face. Upon meeting his gaze, I felt an overwhelming shame. I dealt with it by hastily unbuckling his belt, removing his penis, and putting my mouth around it. Nothing leading up to this moment had prepared me for the confusion I felt. My discomfiture was directly tied to my fear of intimacy. I had never wanted to kiss a boy before, and in my mind, I believed that wanting to kiss a boy was actually what made you gay, not all the dick sucking.

Startled, Noah whispered, "Whoa. What are you doing?"

I didn't have the power to speak or even look at him. He took my chin in his hand and tilted my face up to meet his electric gaze. He then slowly removed his left hand from behind his head to gracefully pull my face toward his. As if buoyed by helium, I ascended. I could feel his soft breath on my face, a mix of cheap malt liquor and marijuana, and meekly lifted my eyes to meet his. Noah then kissed me in earnest, and in that moment, I came flying out of the closet.

Our friends burst through the stairwell door, laughing. It turned out that Noah had made a bet with my friends that he could get me to come out, and who could resist Noah? I should've been indignant, as my coming out was the result of a bet, but I didn't have any time to care. I was awakened to feelings. I had endured sixteen years without them. I had tortured many girlfriends with obligatory nonemotions, while I'd carefully stifled any intimacy that could have blossomed between Kurt, Jordan, and myself.

I thought about Noah constantly. I spent every waking moment enjoying my new freedom. I came out as though I had pioneered homosexuality. With a drop-dead-gorgeous senior on my arm, I was emboldened, and I flaunted my gayness like my cat flaunts her anus. He took me shopping at the Salvation Army while the rest of my schoolmates shopped at Abercrombie & Fitch. I was proud of the silver-glitter, secondhand Sauconys I found and a T-shirt that had an iron-on glitter appliqué of a frog that said, "I'm so happy I could just shit." My teachers always made me turn it inside out when I wore it, and I'd call them homophobic.

Noah and I would often drive around listening to Ani DiFranco in his dusty-blue, late-eighties Toyota and park somewhere to blow each other before he'd drop me off at home. One fateful afternoon, he pulled into my driveway to drop me off, and we noticed my mother's car was not there. We figured she was out and continued making out in the driveway until we saw my mother's shell-shocked face in the kitchen window. She bolted to the door and opened it, her yellow, dish-gloved hands still dripping with hot water and Palmolive, and shouted, "JAMES BRUCE WHITESIDE, GET YOUR ASS IN HERE!"

Terror shot through my body in the form of adrenaline. This was a moment of true horror. I'd have preferred an axe murderer any day. Being caught in the act is petrifying for any teen, but for a queer teen, it's a slow and agonizing death, like having your nose hairs plucked out one by one and then sprinkled over your last meal.

I marched myself up the steps and into the house. I squeaked, "That's Noah. He's my boyfriend." And then I ran to my room and locked the door. I blared Fiona Apple as my mother pounded on the door, demanding that I come out and talk to her. I did not oblige. Perhaps it's a blessing that she saw us that day. Who knows when I would've mustered the courage to actually come out of my own volition.

Later that night, my mother asked me to talk. Things had cooled down a bit and I timidly stepped out of my room. She said, "Family meeting," and led me into the living room, where my stepfather waited for us. She sat me down in a chair and began a denial-laden diatribe that was so traumatic I actually remember very little of it. She said she didn't want me to get AIDS and die, as some of her friends had. I sat in the chair as she bawled, "I DON'T WANT YOU TO DIEEEE!"

I was mute and immobile. It was just like a World War II movie after a bomb went off; like the sound had been sucked out of the room and all that was left was a dull, high-pitched ringing in my ears that vaguely resembled my mother's voice. Every now and then I'd glance from my mother's pain-racked face to my stepfather's concerned one. Had I ruined my family? I liked my family. I didn't want to break them, but I had finally felt feelings. I finally felt like everybody else, even though what I felt made me feel nothing like anybody else. I hugged them both, saying nothing, and retreated to my room.

In the coming weeks, my mother tried to get more information out of me, but I was very loyal to my silence. She even suggested I date Beyoncé, as if we were buddies and went to the same high school. "You like Beyoncé, right? Why don't you date her?" As I was doing my homework and watching *Sailor Moon*, she'd come regale me with stories of people who'd gone through this gay phase. One afternoon, I became more irascible than usual and interrupted her, shouting, "I AM A BIG ... FUCKING ... FLAMING ... FAGGOT!" She told me not to curse and shut the door quietly.

While I was at home, I was a tensed-up ball of stress. Every interaction had the potential to lead to a "serious talk" of which I wanted no part. Verbalizing emotion is damn hard, and I did not yet have the tools to do so. I felt like an infant who didn't yet have the words to say, "I would now like to take a nap, please." So I just huffed and stomped and screamed bloody murder into my pillow while blasting angsty chick rock. It felt good at the time, though I know it was doing nothing for my emotional intelligence. Emotional tantrums are like silent-but-deadly farts. You're glad you got it out, but boy, do they stink.

Noah and I dated for a while, until he told me he was no longer interested. I came to find out later that he was already sleeping with my friend Max. Teenage heartbreak feels like being torn asunder. Aging whittles down the impact of intense life events, breakups, tragedies, deaths, until you're so familiar with the feelings that you gain power over them, accepting them as part of the whole "I'm alive" schtick. But as a teen, I was destroyed. Decimated. Razed. I made a tormented, ironic piece about it in art class. The background was a watercolor prism of rainbow colors that I washed in water so the colors dripped down. On top of this sloppy, depressing rainbow, I drew a man and a woman. That's how rooted I was in my self-loathing. The man was sitting on the ground with his hands around his legs and his chin resting upon his knees. Above him was a woman lying on a cloud amid a starry sky, reaching down to him with her right hand. On plastic film in calligraphy over the drawing, I meticulously quoted Fiona Apple. I wanted this piece to be amusing, but it was just melancholy. I still have it.

I asked myself, "Without Noah, am I still gay? Can homosexuality be limited to one person?" I became lonely and confused. Pre-Noah, I had felt powerful by using denial as a flotation device. Now I was sinking into loneliness, mired in my own bewilderment and doubt. What had once made me feel special now made me feel alienated. Were any of those feelings of true desire worth the torture I now felt? Was belonging to the norm better than being oneself?

Soon after our breakup, I developed a sore throat and a fever. I brought it to the attention of my mother, who, as a nurse, quickly informed me I must have gotten herpes from my gay boyfriend. She took me to the doctor's office where she worked and had me tested for all sorts of things, convinced I was riddled with STIs. Turned out I simply had strep throat and was given antibiotics. She didn't apologize or try to explain herself. I'll never forget the way she looked at me as she dragged me to her Dodge Caravan, shouting that her sixteen-year-old son had herpes and God knew what else from his gay boyfriend. I learned quickly the effects of stigma.

My confusion finally waned when I met a boy named Sean who went to my high school. He was short and stocky, with a wide nose and crooked teeth. I found his personality and bad posture endearing. He wore Aéropostale, which is what people who couldn't afford Abercrombie & Fitch wore. You can't spell it without the word *stale*. Sean was fun and friendly and very in the closet, which didn't stop me from developing a crush on him. Facing my feelings for him further solidified my place in the hall of homosexuality.

Despite all my crushing and weird teenage flirting, Sean didn't come out to me in high school. A decade later, though, I ran into him in the restroom of a gay club in Boston. I screamed, "I KNEW IT!!!" as I washed my hands and he quickly dashed out of the restroom.

IN THE YEAR 2000, I went to ballet boarding school in Virginia, foreswearing my Connecticut roots in search of a more unbridled, Southern bigotry. During winter break, I went home to visit my family. My friend Jeremy, who was the gayest person I had ever met at that time, invited me to his New Year's party at his apartment in Alphabet City in Manhattan. By this point I had completely surrendered to my ferocious gayness, wearing cutoffs and crop tops, lisping unashamedly, and piercing my tongue with a blue marble barbell. I wore glitter and metallic fabrics exclusively, and I was a mincing thorn in my mother's Greenwich-raised side. Jeremy's party looked exactly like a teenage New York New Year's Eve party in 2000 should: wine coolers, Jell-O shots, lamé, and wide-leg, low-rise jeans.

Early in the evening, I ran into Max, the interloper who had sealed my fate with Noah. When the ball dropped, Max and I looked at each other, nodded, and walked out into the hallway together. "There's a bathroom over here," he said, looking over at a communal bathroom. We stripped and got in the shower together. I recall removing my tongue piercing to perform fellatio. This act felt like a final fuck you to my first love, as if I were saying, "He doesn't just want you. He wants

DIAGRAM OF A GAY
PUBESCENT MILLENNIAL

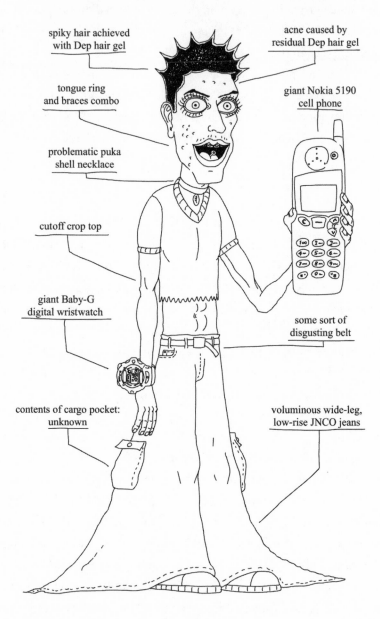

spiky hair achieved
with Dep hair gel

acne caused by
residual Dep hair gel

tongue ring
and braces combo

giant Nokia 5190
cell phone

problematic puka
shell necklace

cutoff crop top

giant Baby-G
digital wristwatch

some sort of
disgusting belt

contents of cargo pocket:
unknown

voluminous wide-leg,
low-rise JNCO jeans

me, too!" I was hooking up with Max to make myself feel better about the break with Noah. Though Max was very attractive, it was not terribly satisfying. I learned that sex cannot be used to erase anguish.

The nail in the coffin of my heterosexuality arrived with a return to its origin. During spring break of 2001, I went back to Connecticut to find that Noah had become a beekeeper, and Max-the-interloper had moved to Washington, DC. I hadn't spoken much to Kurt and Jordan in two years; we had fallen out of touch, as kids tend to do. I called Jordan and asked if he wanted to hang out. He invited me over. I drove up to his house, the same house in which I'd had my first homosexual experience, feeling the anticipation streaming hot in my veins.

His parents weren't home. We spoke somberly and quietly, not quite sure how to bridge the distance that had grown between us. We played a computer game upstairs in the home office for a while. I recall the atmosphere of the cozy Connecticut study in the late evening, with the floodlight from the garage peering severely through the slatted windows. I remember studying his pale face in the film-noir light, how his beard was coming in, how his hair was longer than it had ever been in the past. I thought, while looking at his soft lips, that I had wasted years not kissing them, when, out of nowhere and everywhere all at once, without taking his eyes off the screen, he said, "Wanna hook up?" Jordan identified as straight, and still does, but what teen can resist liberal, magnanimous sex?

I said, "Sure." We undid our pants and gripped each other's already erect penises, as though we knew it would come to this. Everything was the same and everything was different. I was myself, the same self I had always been. I was my number one fan and my own worst enemy. It was acceptance that was the difference.

He said, "You're gay now?"

"Yup," I whispered.

He said, "This is the last time we can do this."

And I replied, "I know."

A BOOM BOX AND A
BOX CUTTER

When I read fiction like Hanya Yanagihara's devastating and relentless *A Little Life*, it makes me furious. How could someone invent such merciless horror? Then I realize that horror is at the crux of simply existing. Tragedy has the power to bolster relationships, test virtuosity, and inspire great, feeling wisdom. It's never for nothing, even though *fair* is an elusive nonsense word we spend our entire lives hunting.

As a gay man, I have experienced much bigotry and violence, though never as much as many others in our country who don't have the ashamedly real benefits of being a white, cisgender man. I find American society ironic because it often talks the talk of inclusiveness and diversity but rarely actually walks the walk. If America claims to be the home of the free, then why is it free only for some?

THE YEAR 2002 was my first as a professional ballet dancer, and the first year I encountered real violence. I had just left the comforts of my mother's home in Fairfield, Connecticut—where the worst brutality I had experienced was the kind of insidious psychological pre-internet bullying that was the white American teenager's most deft skill—and moved to Boston's South End with one of my new Boston Ballet co-workers. In 2002, I was eighteen, and the South End was gay and lovely. Now, naturally, the young families have moved in, blocking every doorway and sidewalk with double-wide, Jeep-size strollers. That's really how neighborhoods evolve: from poverty to the homo-sexuals to the young families with too much money.

One evening, one of my coworkers invited my roommate and me to a party at her place in Roxbury. She rented a room from Paul Thrussell, who was then a principal dancer. I idolized Paul's dancing and also had a crush on him. Leave it to me to have a crush on the reigning champion of the company. Power and talent have always been sexy to me. What does that say about me, I wonder? I used to stand behind him at the ballet barre during class, and if he moved spots, I'd follow him to his new location. I was a little gay puppy, sniffing out talent and a formidable Snausage.

This was my first time at a principal dancer's home, and I was nervous. I imagine I was twitchy and strange, giggling at a high pitch while spilling my Tang-and-vodka mix. Paul flirted with me the ac-ceptable and requisite amount, enough to egg me on without inspiring me to action. All in all, it was a fabulous party, filled with beautiful people and talented artists.

When it was time to go home, the apprentices made their exit en masse. Many of us lived in the South End or in Back Bay, so we decided to take the T, which is Boston's subway. Roxbury had a reputation for being dangerous, but we were filled with the boldness of youth. Trains in Boston come once every seventeen hours, it seems, and so we waited on the platform for quite a while, giggling over the night's incredulities. My soon-to-be boyfriend, Mason, took out his Discman, which was loaded with Mariah Carey's *#1's* album. We sat on a bench, one earbud in each of our ears, and snickered at Mariah's high notes in "Emotions."

There was a gentleman on the other side of the bench who scooted around to sit next to me. He appeared to be in his mid-thirties and intoxicated, with yellowed eyes and breath that smelled sweet and sour. He wore drab clothes that hung limply off his gaunt, ashen frame. Leaning close to me, he asked, "Will you put batteries in my boom box?"

I wondered if that was some sort of unpleasant euphemism, but then he then held up an impossibly banged-up black boom box, its metal speaker cages dinged, scratched, and abused from years of torture.

Mariah still whistling in my ear, I stammered, "N-no, thank you."

He then leaned closer and held up a handful of D batteries. His hands were cracked and calloused, and his finger pads strained white as he clutched the power cells as if they were a fistful of Hope diamonds.

"Just put the batteries in."

"No-no, thank you."

"Why won't you do it?"

"Why can't *you* put them in?"

"Just put the fucking batteries in."

"I . . . I'm sorry. No, thank you."

"What the fuck do you mean, 'No, thank you'?"

I stood up slowly. The belligerent man also stood and began swaying in place. Mason and I tensed and cautiously backed away. He began to shout, "What the fuck?! Just put the MOTHERFUCKING BATTERIES IN!" Like a zombie, he shuffled toward me. I was frozen in place. Mason had abandoned me for the safety of the group of our friends.

"You're not welcome here," the man said to me. I wasn't sure if he was referencing my homosexuality, my race, or both. "You're gonna die tonight," he added, hissing through crooked, graying teeth.

I turned around and power-walked up the stairs to the station's entrance, where a booth housed the station clerk behind bulletproof glass. I said to her through the tiny metal intercom, "Pardon me, ma'am. There's a nice gentleman on the platform saying he's going to kill me. Would you kindly call the police?"

She told me she would and instructed me to wait at the edge of the platform until the train came, then to board, so I descended the stairs.

When I returned to the platform, the man had accosted my friends. I could hear his performative speech. "He thinks he's a tough guy, huh? Well, he's gonna die tonight. I'm gonna kill him. Would you like some candy?" He pulled out a fistful of plastic-wrapped candies from his cargo pant pocket. I wondered if it was really candy. My friends, shaking with fear, each took a small piece.

"YOU KNOW WHAT I DO FOR A LIVING?" he kept shouting. "I LAY CARPETS. I CUT THEM UP! LIKE I'M GONNA CUT UP YOUR FRIEND, THE TOUGH GUY!"

By then, I was absolutely peeing myself a bit, and I hustled back up the stairs to the negligent station clerk. I rasped, "Where are the police? Why aren't they here yet?!"

"They're on their way. It takes awhile." I don't believe she ever truly called them.

From upstairs, I heard the distant rumbling of the train careening through the tunnel and gathered my waning fortitude. I whisked myself down the long stairwell, planning to jump quickly onto the train, only to be greeted at the base of the stairs by the man, gray teeth flashing in a steely grimace, eyes rabid and crazed, holding the boom box in one hand and brandishing a monstrous, serrated utility knife in the other.

The knife itself became an entity all its own. It was fiendish and diabolical. The man vanished and all I could see was my fear reflected in the beveled edges of the device of my demise.

The double doors to the first train car sprang open and I took my chances, throwing my weight to the left and disappearing into the train. I ran through the cars with the fire of terror surging through my veins, my face a taut mask of effort. My breath was short and ragged as I shot beads of spittle into the stale public-transport air. I ran without looking back. I heard the cries and shrieks of surprise in my wake as I tore past strangers. I heard the shouts of my friends, their tormented sobs of terror. My lungs burned. I was a rabbit narrowly avoiding the snarling, snapping maw of a wolf, my fear surging through me in the assistive form of adrenaline. I thought about how much it felt like being onstage. I wondered if it would hurt, if he'd kill me quickly, or make me bleed out slowly. I registered the colors flashing past me, the cozy winter coats of strangers. I saw their eyes widen in alarm, showing the full circles of white surrounding their irises as they registered my situation. I saw the breath catch in their throats, mouths slowly falling agape, unable to say or do anything to help. It all happened so fast. I was the afterimage of a flash of lightning. I was eighteen years old and in no mood to be gutted by a madman.

The doors to the train never closed, as the conductor had most likely been made aware that there was a scuffle onboard, and I burst back out of the train from the final car. I could still hear the guttural shouts from the man behind me, his belligerent battle cry. My only way out was back over the platform and up the stairs. There was also a long escalator that, in a split second, I decided to take, two steps at a time, until I arrived at the station clerk's booth. I hid behind it, as far away from the man's point of view as possible. From my hiding spot I heard a dull thud followed by a sharp clang and a succession of pachinko-like dings—his boom box, tumbling from his viselike grip, clattering down the escalator steps.

My demon pursuer crested the top of the escalator, shouting, "YOU'RE NOT WORTH IT. You're not worth it." After rescuing his beloved, nonworking boom box from the bottom of the escalator, he casually pushed through the turnstiles and sauntered through the station's swinging doors. I could hear his devolving utterances as he made his way down the street. "Not . . . worth . . . . it."

The clerk banged on the bulletproof glass from within her impenetrable fortress and said to me through the box, "They held the train for you. Go get on it. The police will find him."

I trepidatiously descended the staircase and boarded the train. My friends were all there on a row of seats, sobbing uncontrollably. I sat down mutely, clearly in shock. Still out of breath, I gazed into the faces of the other riders as they swayed with the train's movements. I read horror on every stranger's face. I knew I was alive by only a hairbreadth. Surviving an assault is one thing; surviving your survival is another matter entirely. The fear follows you wherever you go.

A train conductor instructed me to file a police report by phone when I returned home, as cell phones at that time were only for Agent Scully or the very rich. I remember sitting on the closed toilet seat in my apartment, holding the beige, curly corded phone receiver to my ear. I was still quietly shaking, not a violent convulsion, but an insidious tremor. I thought to myself how perfunctory the call was. How there wasn't a hope in hell of discerning my attacker from anyone else with a boom box, which was not an uncommon accessory at the time. The futility fueled my self-pity, but also made the whole night seem morbidly funny.

THE FOLLOWING YEAR, I moved into an apartment in Boston's Irish Catholic neighborhood, South Boston, also known as Southie. I couldn't afford my South End apartment any longer on my $300-per-week salary. I roomed with a young dancer named Joel, who would later end up being my personal trainer in New York City. He always tells everyone that when we were roommates, he'd come out of his bedroom in the morning to find me in the kitchen wearing high heels and an apron, making eggs and screaming along to Cher on the CD player. A falsehood, but an undeniably chic one.

Southie wanted nothing to do with me. I was a scrawny nineteen-year-old homosexual ballet dancer thrust into the religious lion's den. My traumatic experience with the man and the boom box had changed the way I existed in public. Every person I passed was someone who could possibly murder me. They'd morph into scary charcoal line drawings with gnashing, knifelike fangs. If anyone moved toward me, I'd startle. If I felt a presence behind me on the street, I'd cross it. I kept my eyes glued to my shoes for fear that anyone should meet my gaze and discern my sexuality. Boston Ballet's music director accosted me one day: "You've got to look where you're going! Why are you always looking at your shoes!"

It wasn't just in my head, though. The violence continued. On my daily walk from the bus to my apartment in Southie, various strangers would hurl slurs and insults at me ad nauseum. "FAGGOT! HOMO! DIE, FAG!" they'd scream, accompanied by shouts of glee and laughter. They'd comment on my clothing, too, shouting things like, "GOD HATES YOUR SHOES!" I recall one incident in which a group of gentlemen gathered stones from a sidewalk garden and threw them at me from behind during my entire walk home from the bus. I silently endured it as rocks relentlessly dinged off my skull, my headphones still on, though I'd paused the music so as to hear any sudden advances without telegraphing my terror. Another scene comes to mind in which a large pickup truck slowed down to pull up beside me, the flatbed full of beer-chugging numbskulls who took turns hucking empty beer bottles at me. They goaded me with tropey lines like "DO FAGGOTS DRINK BEER IN HELL?!" as they sprayed me with shaken beer, performing an abusive homoerotic malt bukkake on the Catholic streets of South Boston.

As a result of all of this I decided to move back into the gay-friendly South End, regardless of how expensive it was. I'd join my friends at restaurants and subsist on bread or tortilla chips. I recall an instance at California Pizza Kitchen in which I growled in my best Batman voice, "GIMME SOME MORE BREAD!" without realizing that our waitress was right behind me. She, completely terrorized, whispered hurriedly, "I'll get it right away, sir!" My friends laughed so hard they cried, and I was absolutely mortified.

One of my Boston apartments was located in the adorable and cozy Bay Village. My best friend Lia lived a few houses down the street. She had a boyfriend named Sam whom we all took turns being mean to for no reason. We had formed the kind of *Mean Girls* clique that everyone hated. Being kind is a choice—a choice it's taken time for me to make. I recommend making the choice sooner than later.

One evening, after a night out at a very douchey nightclub/restaurant called Mantra, Sam, Lia, our other friends, and I all walked back to Bay Village. I was powering up my computer and making a cup of Sleepytime tea when I heard strange, successive popping sounds outside. I didn't think much of it, but a few moments later I received a harried call from Lia. She sounded manic. "Sam's been shot. He's bleeding out on the stoop. I called 9-1-1. They're coming."

I ran out of my apartment barefoot, tearing down the street as sirens blared and red and blue lights flashed in a frenzied way. The ambulance had arrived, and they were moving Sam onto a gurney. Lia was hysterical, sobbing and clutching her mother, who was visiting at the time. I was speechless. I had never seen so much blood. I silently stood there in my flannel pajama bottoms as my best friend's boyfriend, whom we all treated horribly, bled out from a gunshot wound. My face was slackened and gormless, but my heart was dashing against my ribs violently.

I spent the next twenty-four hours in the emergency room with Lia and her mother. Sam was in surgery to close up the gaping wound in his abdomen. It was as though we were in a horrifying Boston spinoff of *The O.C.*, a teen drama we watched and loved in which insane things happened to rich white people in Southern California.

The violence in our lives not only affected the way I interacted with the outside world, it also affected the friendships I had built. Sam's inexplicable drive-by shooting coincided with a time during which my other best friend, Prince, wouldn't speak to me as a result of years dealing with unrequited feelings. Prince was in the hospital with us, too, and I recall sitting across from him as the machines hooked up to Sam's convalescing body beeped and ticked away between us. It was the first time we had spoken for quite some time. Shortly after this, Prince and I mended our friendship. It turns out that petty youthful dramas are often resolved by someone getting shot.

These experiences have inspired me to be inclusive and kind, traits I was not born with. Inspecting the way these incidents linger in the recesses of my mind motivates me to cultivate my sense of empathy, and also my sense of resilience. Things may *happen* to you, but you have to try like hell to *happen the fuck* back to them. Think of it as vengeance for good—using your heart, soul, and latent righteousness to win the war against life's infallible cruelty. *Winning* is the wrong word. Learning to persevere is the true triumph.

DICK COLLEGE

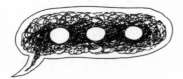

I was eighteen years old when I moved to Boston to join Boston Ballet's apprentice company, Boston Ballet II. Dating in Boston was like going to Dick College. I arrived not knowing what I would major in; I just knew it was my dream school. Over the years, I whittled down my interests until I knew a bit more about what I wanted. I failed so many tests and made myriad enemies until I met a gentleman named Dan, later known to most as Milk the drag queen. Sadly, after twelve years together, we parted ways. And though I'm still wandering the musty halls of Dick College, searching, each passing course helps to give me the knowledge I need to find my major.

MASON

Being thrust into ballet company life as an eighteen-year-old is like wearing a sign that says, "Wanna bang?!" I was struck by the confident way in which people were homosexual in the company. There were so many handsome male dancers, all the way up to around forty years old, as well as a "totally would" ballet coach.

BBII was home to three homosexuals: myself, Logan, and Mason. The company arranged for me to live with Logan in a modest two-bedroom in Boston's South End, which was considered a gayborhood. What a boon! I was excited to move away from home, but nervous about living with someone I hadn't met.

My fears were put to rest as soon as I met Logan. He was a tall, lanky late teenager with Grecian curls and cheekbones that would make Cher jealous. His lips were full and pursed, with eyebrows that seemed meticulously plucked while remaining expansive. I marveled at those brows. It was as if every hair had been brushed and gelled into place, fanning up, up, and away from his large eyes. Logan wasn't particularly effeminate, but his tastes in popular culture betrayed his homosexuality. We became fast friends—fast best friends. I owe much of my gay history knowledge to him.

Mason—or as I like to call him, Mason—was a ballet prodigy trained at New York City Ballet's School of American Ballet. He was short and muscular, and quite burly and hairy for a teenager. His hair was worn straight and long, in a pre-Bieber mop. His eyebrows were plucked into Pamela Anderson arches, and he had long, exposed teeth. He had a rear end like you wouldn't believe. Like if Kim Kardashian, Jennifer Lopez, and Cardi B Frankensteined a butt. Isn't that what rich people are now? Just Frankenstein's monsters?

Mason had an incredible "facility." That's what dancers call a body conducive to ballet, though it sounds more like a bathroom or a building. His torso was short, his knees were hyperextended, and his feet were beautifully arched.

As our friendships blossomed, so did amorous feelings. I recall lying on the sofa one night while Mason massaged my feet and Logan massaged my shoulders. It was the first time in my life I'd been caught between two suitors. I had always been the one begging boys to love me. But there came a point at which I was forced to choose. Logan or Mason?

You know what never occurred to me? That I could choose *neither.* That I could continue to enjoy being single. This sums up youth; the avoidance of conflict only brings more conflict. I assumed turning down one suitor would be easier than turning down both. Talent attracts me and great dancing is a huge turn-on, so I chose Mason. Logan bore the news silently and stoically, with no efforts to change my mind. He casually slipped back into the friend zone as one slips into cozy pj's.

Mason and I moved into a one-bedroom in Boston's South End together after a year of dating. We were often competing for the same roles. I don't believe I was seen as much of a threat at first, but in time, my director and choreographers began to give me big chances, while Mason was overlooked.

I don't think I was ever attracted to Mason outside of his dancing. That's not to say he's not a good-looking guy; I just didn't know what I liked yet. But that's what dating is for, isn't it? To figure out who you *don't* want to fuck? We had many awkward conversations about our sex life, sitting on the mattress on the floor of our bedroom. He would say things like, "You think I'm ugly," which reflected more on what he thought of himself than what I thought of him. He was absolutely adorable, but I just didn't feel that undefinable spark. He also accused me of being selfish and too aggressive in my pursuit of a successful career in dance. He was right. I was too afraid to say anything that might hurt his feelings, and as a result, I was so elusive that I tortured

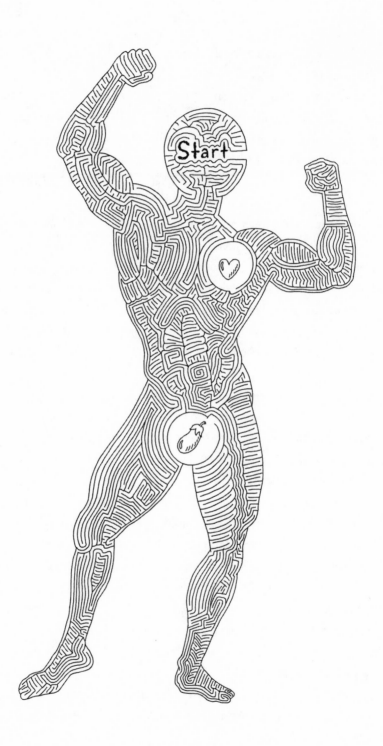

him. I was a complete horror and feel remorseful about the way I handled things.

I eventually found the courage to break up with Mason. We slept in the same room, in beds on opposing walls, for half a year. Man, what an awkward time. I knew he hated me (still hates me), but neither of us was in a financial position to move out. I'd lie down on my twin bed in the dark Boston night feeling his electric revulsion aimed at me until I drifted off to dolorous slumber. I'm sorry, Mason. I was horrible.

MYSPACE DATING

When I was twenty, there was an amazing website called Myspace. It was the bastard child of AOL, geared at horny early-aughts internet users. One could create a profile, "friend" people, search local users, join groups, assign music to one's page, and create a Top 8 friends list. All in all, it was another way to feel alienated while pretending you're making friends.

At the time, cell phones only made phone calls and sent rudimentary text messages, composed using the keypad of your phone. There was no Grindr. I repeat, there was no Grindr! As a gay man under the age of twenty-one, where the hell was I supposed to find a date? Or a lay, for that matter?!

Enter Myspace.

I had a string of Myspace victims. The first person I went on a date with after breaking up with Mason was a Bulgarian college student named Orlin. He invited me to a Harvard mixer and I agreed to join him. I was very out of my element at Harvard, because I had barely graduated from high school and felt inadequate. (Ironically, a decade or so later, I would return to Harvard as a participant in Harvard Business School's Crossover into Business program. Hair flip.)

Orlin was about nine feet tall, with very plucked eyebrows. I don't know why the eyebrow pluckers flocked to me. He had acne-scarred cheeks and the oiliest skin I've ever seen. I have oily skin, but Orlin was a glassy mirror. He was nice, but we had zero chemistry. I still don't think I had met anyone I really wanted to have sex with yet, other than my seventh-grade science teacher, Mr. Dillon, who was ex-Army and wore tight polo shirts, close-cropped hair, and pleated khakis, and would press his junk up against the lab tables while lecturing. Orlin didn't stand a chance.

Next was another Myspace guy named Michael Anthony, a philosophy major at Harvard. He was very short and had a great face. I was almost attracted to him, but I found him insufferable. I enjoy philosophy, just not twenty-year-old philosophers.

During the time I was seeing Michael, my friends and I hosted a "Disney Princess Power Hour" party in which I cut sixty Disney songs down to one minute each and spliced them together to make an hour of brilliant nostalgia porn. Each time the song changed, one was required to drink. One famed drink we created was called a "Tangula." It consisted of Tang, vodka, and peach schnapps, and we sometimes made it as an icy blended beverage with a Tang rim. The hangovers were incredible. Another blended dumpster fire was the "Dirty Girl Scout," and it called for Baileys, vodka, and Thin Mint Girl Scout Cookies. Our Disney Princess party was not only a drinking party, it was a costume party. We wore whatever we had that made us feel like princesses.

Michael Anthony and his friend showed up in skimpy tennis garb. I was not sure of its application to our theme. While my friends and I reenacted scenes from *The Little Mermaid* and *Aladdin*, they sat dourly on the sofa. Michael Anthony's friend had tucked his feet up preciously so that his testicles were hanging out the side of his tennis shorts. My friends and I were mortified and confounded by his lack of humiliation. We were singing along to "Part of Your World," getting sloshed, and giggling at a stranger's nut sack. Shortly thereafter, I sacked Michael Anthony. Nuts.

My next victim, JR, was a fine-boned, effeminate thing with beautiful eyelashes, like a pretty doe. I wasn't into him. Then there was one my friends nicknamed "Butter Tooth" because he was butter soft and his teeth had been whitened so much that they looked silver. I brought him back to my apartment after a night out. We were making out and he was trying to remove my belt (I wore a belt in those days). He tried and tried but couldn't get the damn thing undone, so I dismissed him.

Phil was a sweet gentleman, a quiet, corn-fed beefcake who studied at MIT. He was one of the first people I was truly attracted to. Unfortunately, he wasn't that into me. He ignored me, and I got the point. I heard a year or two later that he had died of a drug overdose at a circuit party.

My final Myspace venture was named James. I refused to date a person named James because that's insane, so I called him Jimmy. He was six foot five and pale as a ghost, with a handsome face and good proportions. He was a graphic-design student and seemed intelligent. It turns out that being intelligent and acting intelligently are two very different things. Nevertheless, I liked him very much. In hindsight, I think I just wanted to have sex with him. Isn't that what "liking" someone means, when you're in your early twenties?

I was now twenty-one or twenty-two, and until that point I hadn't really had sex with anyone. I had enjoyed plenty of hookups, laden with heavy petting and foreplay, but no good old-fashioned intercourse. I behaved as though I were this sexual goddess, when in fact I was a prude, a puritan. Jimmy was the first guy I really wanted to have sex with. Anal intercourse is kind of scary. I poop out of there!!!

But where there's a Jimmy, there's a way. He spent a week essentially living at my apartment, as school was out and he didn't want to go back to his parents' house somewhere in northern Massachusetts. This was essentially when I lost my virginity. I was the top, a Lilliputian mounting a giant of a man. It was fine—nothing to write home about, as virginity losses tend to be underwhelming.

We kept seeing each other intermittently until one fateful day when I went to visit him at his parents' house. We played *Halo* and made out in his room. But when it was time for me to drive back to Boston, there was a blizzard looming. Jimmy's parents invited me to stay over, but my ballet guilt kicked in. "I can't!" I told them. "I have rehearsal!" Waving goodbye to Jimmy, I got in my little beige 1995 Toyota Corolla, which I had named "Showbiz."

It was already coming down something fierce when I left their driveway. By the time I got on the highway, it was whiteout conditions. I was listening to Janet Jackson's *All For You* album and talking to a friend on my new, ultraslim Nokia phone when Showbiz began to drift in the blizzard. I was going only about twenty miles per hour, but my little stick-shift tin can began spinning down the Massachusetts highway in search of something to smash into. There was no automatic braking system—computers had not yet been integrated into cars—so my life slowed down into a cinematic time stop, Janet Jackson whisper-singing "Doesn't Really Matter" as I careened in a snowy spiral into a Subaru SUV down the road.

I hit their rear bumper with my driver's-side headlight, and Showbiz crunched up. The SUV was completely unscathed, not even a ding. I was able to get out of my car and carefully approach the SUV to maniacally ask if everyone was OK. "We're fine," the driver and passenger said, "but your car is not." Then they drove away.

I was sitting in my dead car, in a Massachusetts blizzard, when the tow truck arrived. The intimidating tow truck man told me, "It's totaled. I can drive you into town, but that's it." The town was Wilmington.

"But I don't have any friends in Wilmington," I whined.

"Not my problem," he said. We silently drove to town in his huge truck, with Showbiz dangling off the back like a vagabond's carryall.

He dropped me off at a Dunkin' Donuts, which people from Massachusetts are obsessed with. It was the only thing lit up in the whole town, with Christmas lights adorning every edge, as the blizzard whipped about in the bleak night outside. I called my friend Joel, who owned a large pickup truck, and begged him to come rescue me in Wilmington. Like a saint, he agreed to leave his Boston apartment in the dead of night to drive through a blizzard to fetch me.

I ordered a coffee and a Boston cream doughnut and sat down at a table for the long wait until Joel's arrival. The local radio station was blaring Coldplay's "Fix You," mocking me as I cried into my watery hazelnut coffee under cheerfully blinking Christmas lights.

When I finally told Jimmy what had happened, he texted me that his feelings toward me were platonic. I had to Google what that meant. We never saw each other again.

THE CHICKEN MAN

Finally I decided it was best to leave Myspace dating behind in the Jurassic period. My dear friend Tony, whom we called Teena after his drag name, Nicoteena Patch, was the Samantha to my Charlotte, and he taught me everything I know. He grew up in South Carolina and used a rifle as his first sex toy, inserting the barrel into his Dixie anus. Teena had names for all of his "bops," as he called them: Blue Hat, Lines Meth, Central Park Meth, Old Scary, and Indian Nice Apartment. He had been hooking up with this gentleman he called "Tremont Teacher" and decided Tremont Teacher and I would be a good match, so he introduced us shortly after Jimmy had friend-zoned me.

Tremont Teacher was in fact named Keith. He lived on Tremont Street and was, yes, a teacher. He was shorter than me, with black hair, a vaguely Italian look, and dark chupacabra eyes whose shadowy irises filled almost the whole eye, leaving no room for the whites. He clearly worked out a lot and had a fit, buff body, but unfortunately, he had horrendous posture. Keith waxed his chest and stomach regularly, which left him mottled with red bumps. A cartoon monkey was tattooed on his stomach. He was very attractive but made poor aesthetic choices.

Sex with Keith was like watching a critically acclaimed movie but still not enjoying it. I understood that he was technically hot, but I wasn't attracted to him. We didn't have "that thing," trite as it may be. We never actually had intercourse, even though he desperately wanted to. I was apathetic. It has taken me a very long time to realize that I should not have sex with people I'm not fully attracted to, even though society makes me feel like I should be having sex. Throw gay society in there and you've got yourself a haunting mix.

I don't remember much about my time with Keith, with the exception of two things. We both considered ourselves tops, and, much like Michael Anthony, his fate was decided at a party with my friends. At the time, Boston Ballet was absolutely wild for a costume party, and we went all out for Halloween. I was a brothel madam Wicked Witch of the West that year. Keith didn't have a costume, so I dressed him up. He was terrified of drag and didn't understand it (red flag) so I put him in an appropriately "butch" costume. I dressed him as a chicken, in a tight white shirt and white tights. I had a knit chicken hat complete with googly eyes that I had bought years before in a market in Helsinki, Finland. As a finishing touch, I secured two small red water balloons to an elastic and tied it around Keith's head, effectively making a testicle-like wattle under his chin. My friends hadn't met Keith before, because I knew how vicious they could be, and this really tickled them. "HE'S A GODDAMN CHICKEN!" they squealed.

What on earth as I thinking? How was poor Keith supposed to integrate into my friend group dressed as a chicken? A tiger, maybe, but a chicken?

From that point on, they called him "Chicken Man" and asked me what I saw in him, which I really didn't know. I wanted it to work. I had had such a string of failures that I was so ready for something to work.

He took me to Red Sox games and to a Kelly Clarkson concert. (I preferred Kelly.) He cooked for me. He introduced me to his parents. I really tried with Keith the Chicken Man, but ultimately failed. When I broke up with him, he was truly angry. He had tried quite hard to win my heart, which I appreciated, but not even Kelly Clarkson singing "Behind These Chupacabra Eyes" could produce the desired feelings.

Weeks later, I received a text from Keith saying that we should remain friends and that there were no hard feelings. I went over to his apartment one night for dinner. At first, things were civilized, and we ordered a pizza. But shortly afterward, Keith went off the rails, delivering a vitriolic diatribe about all my many shortcomings and essentially telling me I was a horrible, selfish, shit person. While this may have been true, I certainly wasn't going to hear it from Keith the Chicken Man. I took twenty dollars out of my wallet, dropped it on the floor, whispered, "This is for the pizza," and walked out of the apartment.

MILK

Dick College was grueling. Boston was home to many prestigious universities, but Dick College made them all look like preschool. I struggled, as many do, to find my path, my major.

As it so happened, my major, for a time, was Dan Donigan, a figure skater later turned drag queen named Milk from Syracuse, New York. I met Dan in 2008 at a gay Boston nightclub called the Estate. I was very drunk and called him "Don" all night. We spent twelve years together . . . but that is another story and shall be told another time.

Turns out Dan had frequented my Myspace profile back in the day. Maybe Myspace wasn't so bad after all.

ALL MY PETS ARE DEAD

Growing up in a middle-class family affords one certain luxuries. My mother's house was always inhabited by a mélange of furry ruffians. There, we were a Hallmark family, riding on the backs of enormous golden retrievers and snuggling with floofy kitties. We dodged enormous mountains of feces that settled into high-pile carpets. We slipped on slimy, viscous pools of cat vomit on olive-green linoleum kitchen floors. We loved, tortured, and maimed the plethora of American Family standard-issue furballs that entered the revolving door of my mother's home.

On the other hand, my father's house was home to D-list pets such as gerbils, mice, and a rabbit. Snuggling was absolutely out of the question. I still bear a long white scar and unspeakable trauma from Babs the bunny. Scraping bepooped cedar chips out of a small cage became my lonely pastime. This sums up my dichotomous childhood perfectly: flagrant flippancy versus austere pragmatism.

ALICE

When I was very young, my mother had a beautiful golden retriever named Alice. Living with Alice was like living with Maria von Trapp. Her singsongy benevolence was unmatched. She had her patient au pair schtick down pat. Alice was essentially our mother, and she took care of us five children effortlessly, even without the whistle-wielding, babelicious Christopher Plummer.

I remember Alice getting out of the shower, her paws dripping wet, all six of her nipples completely ravaged by her many children, and turning on the *Today* show while putting her ears up in a Turbie Twist. Once she even asked me, a five-year-old, "How does Katie Couric get her eyelashes so voluminous?"

"Human mascara works so much better than dog mascara," I told her.

Alice was hit by a garbage truck. Or was it my brother who was hit? I don't remember anymore. Alice, however, refused to die, even though she was mauled beyond recognition. My human mother, Nancy, made the call to put our suffering dog/nanny/mother Alice to sleep. Isn't that insane? That we call it putting them "to sleep"? Sleep, by nature, indicates that a creature will wake up. Hell, even Rip Van Winkle woke up. Even Sleeping Beauty! I was faintly sad, as though someone had eaten the last yogurt. It wasn't the same type of devastation that I would feel later, over the death of a pussycat.

MOOKIE

A year or two later, my mother brought home a German shepherd named Mookie, a name that now sounds vaguely racist to me for some reason. German shepherds look like doomsday devices compared with golden retrievers, and I, at six or seven, was wary. I gave Mookie the benefit of the doubt until one night, I awoke to find him sitting next to my bed, the whites of his eyes glowing in the suburban Connecticut dark, the way you'd imagine Jeffrey Dahmer staring at a little boy he was about to rape and dismember. I startled awake and leaped out of my bed, tore down the stairs, and dashed out the door to the backyard with Mookie in vicious pursuit. I could hear his growls. He was saying, "Little boy! Little boy! I'm gonna eat your face!!!"

I had made it to only the middle of the backyard when Mookie tackled me and began snapping at my face, saliva dripping off his menacing jowls. I was screaming bloodcurdling screams when my mother burst from the door and grabbed Mookie's collar, trying to forcibly rip him off me while he kept shouting, "I'm gonna freeze your head for later, little boy!" His teeth caught on my footie pajamas and tore them, exposing my arms to the frigid winter night.

Finally, my mother pinned down the beast and managed to cage him. The next morning, she phoned Animal Control. They picked Mookie up that day and, I imagine, put him "to sleep." No trauma here, though. I'm all good. Fucking fuck. Damn you, Mookie.

CHERRY MERRY MUFFIN

Shortly after Mookie's farewell, on a sunny Connecticut morning, a pristine white cat sauntered onto our back deck. Beholding it with God-fearing awe, I exclaimed, "Michelle Pfeiffer is on our back deck!" My mother decided to investigate. "No collar!" she said happily. We kids knew what that meant. Michelle Pfeiffer was ours now.

My mother had the temperament of a seven-year-old vegan girl who loves ponies. Any animal that wandered up to the door, she'd take in.

Sven, for example, wandered up to our door one day shortly after Michelle Pfeiffer's arrival. Sven—I've no idea why we called him that—was a very befloofed bichon frise with the temperament of a jacked-up coke fiend. Nancy knew that this dog had to belong to some unknown neighbor, but we kept him all the same, until about a week later, when someone knocked on the door and said, "Give me back my dog, you psychopath!" Nancy obliged.

Back to Michelle Pfeiffer. Because I was basically an adorable little girl, my mother let me name the absolutely stunning white pussycat. I decided to name her Cherry Merry Muffin, after a doll that I was desperate to own but would never acquire. This doll had a manic 1980s commercial that aired incessantly during my youth. Little white girls would shout, "SHE BAKED CHERRY MUFFINS FOR HER PARTY!" and "THEY SMELL LIKE CHERRIES!" and "SO DOES CHERRY MERRY MUFFIN!!!" Thus, Michelle Pfeiffer became Cherry Merry Muffin. Who in their right mind bakes muffins for a party? If I had a party and someone brought muffins when I'd asked for vodka, I'd sic Mookie on them.

Cherry Merry Muffin replaced Alice as my caretaker. I loved her more than anything, perhaps even more than television or my mother. She'd mutter glamorous things to me, such as "Let Muffin finish her martini before we go to Hermès" and "My favorite Disney princess is Cruella de Vil."

We played many games together, but our favorite was hide-and-seek. I don't know if you know this, but playing hide-and-seek with a pussycat is like playing hide-and-forget. As we were playing hide-and-seek one day, I "hid" her (from myself) in one of those old wicker flip-top hampers. After hiding Muffin, I shouted, "OK, now it's my turn to hide!" But I was a child with the attention span of a forest stoat. I forgot that I had hidden Muffin in the hamper. A few days later, my mother asked, "Have you seen Muffin?" I squeaked and then ran upstairs to the wicker hamper, where I found the glamorous Cherry Merry Muffin covered in her own piss and shit and yowling at the top of her lungs, "I'M A SHIT MUFFIN! HOW DARE YOU?!"

I have so much guilt surrounding my pets. I was a child, but I don't believe that's an excuse.

Once freed, Muffin decided to explore her sexuality. She'd say to me, "Muffin needs a Friday night," and she'd disappear for the weekend, returning only to receive her Tender Vittles. After one of these sojourns, she got pregnant. As the last of my mother's children, I had not yet seen anything, human or animal, with child. So to see my beloved and chic Cherry Merry Muffin so engorged was horrifying.

"Why is Muffin so fat?" I asked my mother.

"Muffin got married in a Catholic church and had consensual sexual intercourse with her husband, and now they're going to have very spiritually enlightened children," Nancy replied.

Muffin gestated for what seemed like three days, then hid among the Nine West high heels at the bottom of my mother's closet and proceeded to yowl at unimaginable decibel levels. Instead of leaving the poor wretch to give birth in private, my mother laid a towel on her princess-height, king-size bed, placed the shrieking pussycat atop it, and said, "Witness God's miracle!" My brothers, my sister, and I watched as a bloated Cherry Merry Muffin gave birth to approximately one thousand mini muffins. They were allegedly kittens, but I recall them looking more like discarded chicken gizzards. I swallowed back bile and thought to myself that "God's miracle" was gross.

Over the next week, I witnessed the most adorable transformation of my life. The gizzards became hilariously proportioned fuzzy kittens. Their heads were enormous and their tails short and stout. They toddled clumsily over each other. Their cuteness as they mewled and yawned was eye-watering. There's a reason why *smitten* rhymes with *kitten.*

Cherry Merry Muffin was a good mother. She carted her little nuggets around in her mouth and taught them to drink from the water bowl. She brought them to the litter box and taught them to shit with dignity. She taught them to display their anuses with the pride that only short-haired cats know. She'd proclaim to the world, "LOOK AT MY ANUS! ISN'T IT STUNNING?!" It's funny that they're called *pussycats* when they really should be called *anuscats.*

Cherry Merry Muffin went missing for a week or two, during which time we were very distressed. We had all these kittens and needed help taking care of them! Our prodigal pussycat finally returned, looking like a Picasso painting. She had clearly been maimed by some sort of machine—perhaps the same fate as Alice? One of her paws had been squished into two dimensions, she was caked with dried blood, and her tail was bent into an angular question mark, similar to a *Super Mario Bros* question block.

"My beloved Cherry Merry Muffin!" I wailed. "What have those brutes done to you?"

This time, I knew what was coming. Nancy placed the barely moving Cherry Merry Muffin on a towel, perhaps the same one the cat had given birth on weeks earlier, and drove her to the veterinarian's office, where she was "put to sleep." I was devastated. I had loved her, perhaps even more than television or my mother.

THE IN-BETWEENERS

Nancy gave away most of Muffin's kittens, but we kept three: Pirate, Cassidy, and Cleo. I didn't understand gender at that age (perhaps I still don't), so I couldn't tell you if they were boy pussycats or girl pussycats. I liked them well enough, but they couldn't replace the bond I had with Cherry Merry Muffin.

Cassidy unfortunately drowned in the pool before we could find her or him a home. We woke up one morning and said, "Oh, look— Cassidy drowned in the pool." It was an excellent lesson in the grammar and spelling of the word *drown*. While my buffoon classmates consistently said "drownded," I'd smugly reply, "It's 'drowned,' Alexis."

Pirate, so named because he or she could open only one eye, opened his or her second eye a few months after being born. It ruined the name and made me resent her or him. I saw it as a betrayal. "How dare you not live up to your very clever name?" I thought. With two eyes open, Pirate died under my mother's very high bed, of a heart attack or something equally inexplicable to a small child. I was bummed but fairly unfazed.

Cleo lived and died and I remember nothing about it, which is sad, because I adore Miss Cleo and frequently shout while I'm alone in my apartment, "YOU'RE A LIBRA, AREN'T YA, DARLIN'?!"

While the next animal on my journey wasn't a pet, it affected my perception of wild animals and the way I react to them. During the post-Muffin era, we had a trampoline in the backyard. It was one of those paralyze-your-children types without nets or any protective barriers on the sides. My brother Andrew and I adored it and jumped on it daily after school. Like most things in our mother's home, it was poorly tended, so it had incredibly rusted springs, maybe half-missing, and holes here and there that exposed the dead grass beneath. Nevertheless, we jumped on it like mad, not caring when our feet landed in the holes and we ended up submerged to the groin.

I was bouncing on it one day after school when I heard a manic chittering beneath me. I ignored it and kept jumping, but then I landed in one of the holes and a gray blur zipped toward me, hissing and spitting. I extricated my foot in the nick of time. A rabid raccoon had invaded the underside of my trampoline, like a troll under a bridge. I remember its eyes. They resembled Jack Nicholson's eyes in the famous "Here's Johnny!" scene from *The Shining.*

There I was, shrieking intermittently like Shelley Duvall, when Nancy shouted from the kitchen window, "Jimbo! Do NOT get off the trampoline! There's a rabid raccoon underneath it! I've called Animal Control!" (She should have had them on speed dial at that point.) My bloodcurdling cries continued as I watched the little fucker bloodthirstily racing about beneath me, as if the Flash had turned to banditry. I caught glimpses of it in the holes of the trampoline and heard it hissing through a clenched jaw.

One hundred million years later, the Fairfield Animal Control unit showed up, lassoed the little douchebag, carted it away in a paddy wagon, and presumably put it "to sleep." Poor wretch. I never used the dilapidated trampoline again.

GUS & CHLOÉ

By this time, my mother had burned through both divorce settlements, and we were forced to move from our Brady Bunch manor into a tiny cottage. My mother had a knack for ignoring her poorness. She pretended she was a Greenwich socialite till the day she died. Nobody had a flair for fantasy like Nancy. Twice divorced, with three kids out of the house in college or otherwise, it was just her, my brother Andrew, and myself. A sane person would have thought to themselves, "OK, it's time to subsist on bread and water for a while," but instead, my mother said, to our delight, "We're getting a puppy!"

After the Mookie Disaster, Nancy decided to go back to golden retrievers. She took Andrew and me to a breeder in Connecticut. (Pet adoption had not yet been invented.) *Breeder*: what a word! As an adult, I've come to know its many meanings. A dog breeder is someone who churns out purebred dogs by carefully selecting which dogs to lock in a room together. These little doggie bang-fests result in puppies with the desired characteristics of whichever breed the breeder is trying to peddle. I've also heard of mixing breeds—like a goldendoodle, labradoodle, cavapoo, peekapoo pom, poopydoop, stinkydump, and the elusive Bernadette Petersdoodle.

Another meaning of the word *breeder* refers to people who have children upon children upon children. Some people find this offensive. I find it hilarious. The final meaning of the word *breeder* is my favorite. Mainly used in homosexual contexts, it is defined by the beloved Urban Dictionary as someone who blows a load or takes a load up the ass without a rubber. Some people find this offensive. I find it hilarious.

We settled on Gus, an adorable runt. He was the sweetest, kindest, most down-to-earth dog a family could hope for. He loved our family even though we, in true form, barely took care of him. We didn't brush Gus or take him to a groomer, so his hair was left to fall out and cover the floor. There was a wall-to-wall carpet of Gus's hair and a general scent to the home that said, "NOBODY CARES!"

My brother Andrew and Gus really bonded. But it never felt like Gus was really my dog. In fact, he irritated me. It was like having a spouse who was too nice. Gus would return from the office with a bouquet of expensive, tropical blooms and declare, "There's my beautiful wife!" and I'd scream, "Leave me alone!" while crying in a bubble bath. He always wanted to lay his adorable golden retriever head in my lap. Ugh, what a nightmare! How irritating! I'd always hiss at him, "Gus! Why must you vex me so?" What I really wanted was another pussycat.

Nancy, being an enabler, took me to the mall to get a cat. The mall was where cats were made in the early 1990s. I selected a petite calico kitten and named her Chloé. I have no idea where I had heard or seen

the name Chloé, especially with that ridiculous accent on the *e*. It was as if Bette Davis were an eight-year-old boy, living in Connecticut.

Chloé and I got along famously, but what I never expected was that Chloé and Gus would become best friends. They would snuggle together on the sofa all the time. It was outrageously adorable and warmed me to Gus a little bit. Chloé would sit atop Gus's neck and knead at his shoulders, then burrow her face under his ear to sleep. They were the best pets an American family could hope for, and they lived long, cozy lives until they both died of old age. They weren't "put to sleep"—they simply went to sleep and just kept sleeping. I miss them.

MAGGIE

Our next cat belonged to my mother and was a gift from her boyfriend. After a series of failed relationships, she met a nice fella named Paul and they got engaged. On my mother's birthday, Paul presented her with a white Persian cat. My mother named it Maggie. A white Persian cat named Maggie! The woman was insane. Thus, Maggie joined the house with Chloé and Gus, who shunned the newcomer.

Do you know how much work Persian cats are? They're like putting together IKEA dressers every day for the rest of your life. Either you struggle through it yourself or you pay someone else to do it, which my mother absolutely would not or could not do. And so, like many of our pets, Maggie suffered as her needs went unmet. She developed enormous mats of hair that dangled off her like heavy Christmas ornaments. Her eyes produced a steady stream of goo that tracked down her cheeks, making her look like she had just smashed her face into a tub of Vaseline. Feces would cling to the fur on her tail, which she'd wave around like some sort of shit pennant. All in all, I think

Maggie was a sad lady. She didn't like to be petted, because you'd inevitably run into one of her mats, which would tug at her skin, and she'd freak out.

Maggie spent most of her time "meditating," as my mother called it. She'd sit up straight, with her eyes closed, for indeterminate periods of time, rocking back and forth subtly as if thinking, "This is not happening. This is not my life." I could feel Maggie's depression as if there were a real-life Eeyore in the room. It was devastating. She vomited all the time, and as she aged, she went blind and lost control of her bowels and bladder.

The irony is that this tortured beast lived the longest out of any pet our family had. I recall visiting my mother's assisted-living apartment in Shelton, Connecticut, and dodging the little barf piles that had become one with the carpet. My mother had stopped bothering to clean them up. I think she figured Maggie would eat them anyway. Maggie lived to be 942 years old.

CALVIN

During ballet class one day, my mother called me on my new cellular telephone, a delightful Motorola flip phone I had recently purchased from Cingular Wireless. Upon snapping it shut, I'd say, "Snapping turtle," with an effeminate flourish.

She was calling to tell me that Chloé had died. I remember crying quietly in the hallway, which really freaked my friends out. I am not a crier, and if I do cry, it's usually at something inexplicable. The majority of my tears come from cuteness. I smile-wept through the first twenty minutes of *Wall-E*. I couldn't handle the cuteness and beauty. I also sobbed uncontrollably when I saw *A Chorus Line* on Broadway, as well as the thirty minutes after the final curtain. I don't know why, I just did. But frankly, when Chloé died, it made me sad . . . so I cried.

After some time had passed, my mother suggested I get my own cat. By this time, I had realized that pet adoption had been invented after all, and I went to visit the Animal Rescue League of Boston. I was twenty years old and wanted a kitten. I found the fluffy calico male equivalent to Chloé, filled out the paperwork, paid the fifty-dollar adoption fee—which to me, at the time, seemed exorbitant—and took my new kitten home.

I named him Calvin (I have no idea why) and he was so cute he made me cry. I wept-played with my new kitten in the apartment where I lived with my boyfriend at the time. What sort of dumbass moves in with his boyfriend at twenty? Me. I'm that dumbass. Calvin seemed vaguely unwell at the time of his adoption. He had very runny yet crusty eyes. Within a day of his homecoming, he began to have uncontrollable diarrhea. Before we confined him to the bathroom, he ran around leaving little fecal kisses on every surface of the apartment. He was unwell for a few days and then things improved. His eyes uncrusted and his feces solidified. He became a model pet.

Calvin was a sweetheart. He played, he liked to be held, and he loved to snuggle. His favorite place was under the duvet, tucked into my armpit. I, however, was a twenty-year-old monster. I decided that my furniture was too valuable to be scratched up by Calvin (when, in fact, I had found most of it on the streets of Boston) and decided to have him declawed. Declawing is the amputation of the last bone on each toe. This is a source of great guilt for me. I cannot believe I declawed my poor cat. I am still mortified. I was ignorant and foolish.

Calvin recovered physically, but he was never the same. He became listless, moody, and depressed. He was not as affectionate as before the surgery, and seemed to know that I was the cause of his pain. He ceased using his litter box. He began biting. I had maimed and traumatized my cat.

We went on in this way for another year or two. Eventually, with the help of my two best friends, Prince and Lia, I took him to the

ASPCA. When I explained what I had done, they were appropriately horrified. I asked if there was someone who might adopt him, or a compound somewhere that houses tortured beasts. They were appalled by my ignorance. "No one will adopt a cat that bites and does not use a litter box," they told me. "And we could not bring a declawed cat to some magical outdoor compound because it cannot hunt or defend itself. But we can put your cat 'to sleep' for a small fee."

I began crying and ran out of the building, leaving my friends stunned. I was still weeping in a nearby meadow as if I were Sally Field in *Steel Magnolias* when I saw Lia emerge from the building. I knew exactly what was happening. In a way, maybe I left so it *could* happen. She said, "Prince did it. He paid for it." The last sentence really tells you where we were at in our lives. Three friends in their late teens/early twenties, killing a cat, and all we could think about is the fee.

This is one of my life's greatest shames. It makes me hate myself so much I can't stand it. I now give money to the ASPCA every month in futile repentance. That I think throwing money at my guilt can change anything means I really haven't changed at all; at heart, I'm still a selfish twenty-something who'd rather kill his cat than deal with a shitty situation. Perhaps people are the ones who should be "put to sleep."

MS. BIT

That same year, after leaving Paul, my mother was scheduled to move in to a small apartment in Milford, Connecticut. Thrice divorced, she could no longer afford a house. This did not dissuade her from getting another kitten. She adopted a funny-looking, short-haired, black-and-white kitten whom she named Lil Bit, because she was so small. She was a kitten—of course she was small! But as with many situations, my mother had an uncanny prescience, and Lil Bit barely grew any bigger.

What a little freak! She should've been named Lil Freak! She was so small it was hard to tell that she was even a cat and not some sort of pygmy marmoset. Her eyes bulged from her face like she had the blood pressure of a middle-aged sumo wrestler. She had cheeks that looked as though she were smuggling nuts therein for winter. I still call this part of her face her "nuts." It doesn't help that they also resemble adorable little cat testicles. Lil Bit seemed like the most stressed-out cat I'd ever seen. She could move so fast! She'd zip along at ankle height, knocking things over and creating total destruction in her wake.

After the adoption, I received a phone call from my mother in which she feigned distress. "My new apartment doesn't allow pets," she said.

"What about Maggie?" I asked.

"Maggie is barely a cat. Will you take Lil Bit for a few months and then I'll sneak her back into the apartment?"

I begrudgingly obliged. I was doing a guest performance somewhere near Hartford, Connecticut, and we arranged for my first dance teacher, Angie, to deliver the pussycat contraband to me before I returned to Boston. Apparently, Lil Bit wriggled free of her carrier in Angie's car and shot about the interior like a bit of rogue flubber. Angie had to pull over to wrestle the creature back into its bag. When Angie arrived, she was covered in thin scratches, and her clothing was distressed like the garments in a Yeezy fashion show. "Here is your mother's demon," she said. "Enjoy."

When I opened the carrier in my apartment in Boston, Lil Bit ran into the bathroom and curled up behind the toilet into the tiniest black ball of floof imaginable, where she remained for about two days. She could easily have been mistaken for a stray pube. I have a friend who has a name for tumbleweeds of hair on the floor. She calls them "muffice." Isn't that great?

I refused to call her Lil Bit because it made me sound like a five-year-old, so while she was under my care I renamed her Ms. Bit. It tells you she might be single, which I liked.

Honestly, she was the most annoying young cat I ever met. All she did was knock things over. It got to the point where I had to remove everything from every surface, unless it was heavy enough to be safe from being pawed off a ledge. She'd approach an object and then look back at me to make sure I was watching, smirk, and wink before she swiped it off.

Ms. Bit was the only cat I actively disliked. I found her smugness insufferable. She'd strut about, proudly displaying her anus for all the world to see. Her anus was a light gray. It resembled a swollen gray balloon knot and it was constantly mocking me, whispering maliciously, "I'm going to fart while you're eating dinner." Its bloated, sickly pallor practically gave itself a name: Graynus.

My friends went apeshit for Ms. Bit. They loved her and sang her praises. They said, "What a face!" "She's a munchkin!" "I'd purchase a townhouse from her!!!" Meanwhile, Ms. Bit continued haranguing me. She was small, as we have established, yet she had long legs, like Meowmi Campbell. One of my favorite party tricks was to say, "Ms. Bit! Do your model walks." I would then reach under her belly, lift her to her full height, and glide her along the floor, her little legs reaching longingly downward to solid ground. On her face, one could clearly read her "CURSE YOU, HUMAN!" expression.

Her long dancer's legs created a problem, though. While using her litter box, she'd stand on tippy-cat-toe and shoot her urine over the side of the box. I swear she did this on purpose. I'd spy on her as she got into the litter box. She'd rear up to her full height, then tremble as she forcibly ejected urine in a shot-put arc over the side of the box. I was forced to purchase a litter box that had sides high enough for a cheetah.

I gave Ms. Bit a series of nicknames that are befitting: Senator Bit, District Attorney Bit, Lieutenant Detective Bit, Demoness, Nachtmare, and Satan.

After three months, I called my mother and told her, "OK, it's time to take your cat back. She's driving me crazy."

"No, thanks," my mother replied coolly.

I was livid, but not livid enough to try to find her a new home. Something was happening between us. Think of Ms. Bit as the Beast and me as Belle. There may have been something there that wasn't there before.

I began to warm to Ms. Bit's eccentricities, and that ice-cold weasel knew it. She began to curl up on my lap as I read a book. She slept (while continuously passing gas) beside the mouse pad as I composed pop music. She helped me fold the laundry and taught me how to do my taxes.

Ms. Bit became my child. And I owe one great accomplishment to her. On my first date with Dan, aka Milk, I regaled him with tales of Ms. Bit. So effective were they that Dan was crying with laughter for an extended period of time. I thank Ms. Bit for essentially "sealing the deal" for me. Bless that little befurred matchmaker.

Ms. Bit lived to be nearly nineteen, and though she has now passed, I was convinced she was immortal. I had noticed some changes in her old age, though. She had found her voice. My little Christina Aguilera began wailing at six a.m. for food. Her meow was broken and sounded like a fork in the garbage disposal. She moved slowly and her fur displayed pluckable tufts. I could tell which parts were ready to be pulled because they stuck out slightly. I had a neurotic compulsion to pluck the tufts, which was somewhat deranged. She had ceased to use the litter box. We had reached a compromise in which she used pee pads, like the ones used to train puppies. But if I went away for too long, she'd take revenge dumps wherever she liked. She had approximately two teeth left in her odiferous mouth. I'd leave dry food out for her all the time, which she swallowed whole. Her true love in life was Smooth Loaf canned cat food. Smooth Loaf comes in many flavors: chicken liver, salmon face, turkey neck, horse hoof, and walrus nipples. If Ms. Bit lived for one thing, it was her beloved Smooth Loaf.

An elderly cat is much like an elderly human. I loved the old bat, but she wasn't living a terribly happy life at that point. I watched her slow down to the point where she lost all control of her bowels and was walking around in obvious pain, wincing and limping with each step. I stuffed the little witch into her carrier and took her to the veterinarian, who delivered the sad but unsurprising news that she was dying from kidney failure and possible colon cancer, and that it was time for her to be put to sleep. Standing outside on the sidewalk (pandemic protocols did not allow pet owners inside the vet's office) while my beloved Nachtmare was being released from a long, happy life, full of snuggles and Smooth Loaf, I asked myself some questions: Are pets worth it? What do they teach us about ourselves?

I have come to the conclusion that caring for something, whether human or animal, is always worth it. Having pets has taught me horrible things about myself. I am selfish and cruel, but I do have the capacity to change. And I think it's easier to learn about yourself from relationships with animals than relationships with humans. The ethics are simplified. Did you provide? Did you love? Did you accept? Did you sacrifice?

With the passing years, I try to treat people the way I learned to treat Ms. Bit: with love and understanding. This way, when I'm finally put "to sleep," I won't hate myself in the afterlife . . . or whatever.

AL

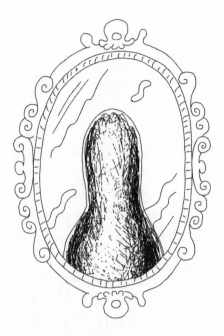

In 1998, a new boy joined my dance studio. His name was Al and he was a year or two older than my friends Kurt and Jordan and myself, who were all fourteen. Al was a charismatic, openly bisexual guy, which fascinated me because I had yet to come to terms with my burgeoning sexuality. He loved to laugh, had a flair for drama, and was seemingly stoned at all times. He wore a silver ball-chain necklace, a look usually reserved for grungy skateboarders. His teeth were bright white, and his hair was fashioned into tight twists, which he absently re-twisted while he emphatically spoke. His face was home to inexplicably persistent specks of glitter—not purposefully applied glitter, but accidental glitter. Perhaps he moonlighted as a teenage drag queen or was often just returning from a club. He sang everywhere he went and dreamed of Broadway stardom.

Al lived in Bridgeport, Connecticut, with his mother. His house had a completely furnished basement, where he'd often host parties at which one could drink forties of Olde English malt liquor, smoke cigarettes or blunts, take ecstasy, and hook up with whoever was interested, all while dancing and singing along to Destiny's Child or TLC. These basement parties attracted people from all over southern Connecticut.

At one of Al's parties, I met a quarterback from Easton, a neighboring town. The quarterback was a stud in classic late-nineties/early-aughts fashion, with spiky frosted tips and a chain necklace peering out of an Abercrombie & Fitch button-down. Later that night, when Al turned off all the nights, the quarterback and I proceeded to hook up right there on the sofa, surrounded by others who had also found hookup partners. I wouldn't kiss him, though. He was the first guy other than Kurt and Jordan I had hooked up with. My fears were beginning to manifest in a real way. Was I gay? At that point, I hadn't really ever kissed a guy, and I hadn't ever had anal intercourse, despite Kurt's best attempts to deflower me using my stepmother's perfumed hand lotion, which only led to an extreme burning sensation in my anus. Fire in the hole! As long as I wasn't kissing boys or having sex with them, I was straight . . . *right?*

During another one of Al's parties, Kurt and I sneaked up to Al's bedroom. We were naked and enjoying ourselves when Al burst into the room screaming, "You're always sucking each other's dicks!!! Why not MINE?! Is it because I'm BLACK?! You're both RACISTS!!!" He was on drugs. I know now that Al was on drugs much of the time. My teenage eyes didn't recognize the signs, though. He was wildly erratic. I know he saw a therapist often and missed rehearsals frequently for unknown mental health reasons.

After his diatribe, Al seized my testicles with one hand, his long

fingernails filed to sharp claws, digging into my scrotum to the point of breaking skin. It felt as if the pressure would rupture one of my testicles. With his other hand, he pressed me down and shouted at me. He put his mouth around my penis and began to bite down, hard. I tried to push him away, but he clamped down harder with his teeth and his long, pointed nails. I honestly don't remember what Kurt did. I just remember thinking that we were too scared to move and that I was in physical pain. Finally, Al released me and abruptly stormed out of the room.

We all remained friends, because teenage boys from Connecticut weren't taught to talk about difficult, real-life situations. I did my best to put it out of my mind afterward. My ability to compartmentalize trauma is one of my *gifts*.

A few years later, I received a call from a friend that Al was found hanging from his bedroom ceiling fan by the cord of a hair dryer. I desperately wanted to feel surprised, but I couldn't muster it. Al was incredibly special, but he was haunted. Sometimes, horror just follows someone you love. Sometimes a bit of that horror rubs off on you, and you wear it at all times, like an outfit you can never change. We have to learn how to be good at accessorizing; otherwise horror is all we see when we look in the mirror.

Stranded in Casablanca:
The Pussycat Dolls Musical

by

James Whiteside

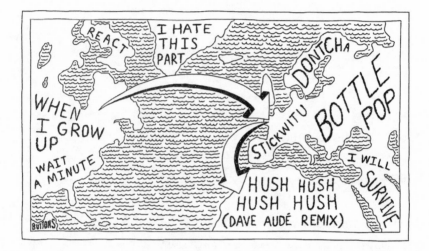

CHARACTERS

JAMES: An American ballet dancer, trying to get home to New
York City. He's hungover from a late night out.

JAMES'S IPHONE: JAMES'S iPhone. Duh.

DAN'S IPHONE: JAMES'S boyfriend Dan's iPhone.

AGENTS, CLERKS, WORKERS, etc.: Airport, hotel, and bar
workers. All played by same man and woman.

ENTITLED RAGE: An Indian businessman prone to fits of rage, trying to get to Boston for work.

CRYING GIRL: A daddy's girl who can't stop crying. A valley girl, spoiled brat, and genius.

QUIET LADY: A quiet lady.

SWEATY WHITE GUY: A nice guy who can't stop sweating.

BRITISH TWINS: Corpulent British twin sisters who curse a lot.

PREPPY: A tall, handsome British man who works in wind energy.

OLD COUPLE: An old couple.

PORTUGUESE SEAMAN: A crude, misogynistic ship officer.

RUPERT: An Irish dancer who was the reason for JAMES'S hangover. Played by same man as PREPPY.

Act One

Scene 1

LONDON GATWICK AIRPORT. 4:01 A.M. CHECK-IN COUNTER.

JAMES, a tall, skinny, bearded homosexual, hurries up to the check-in desk for British Airways. He is dragging two

suitcases behind him and keeps tripping on the wheels, as
the handles aren't long enough for him.

> AIRPORT MAN 1
>
> Check-in is closed.

> JAMES
>
> 'Scuse me?

> AIRPORT MAN 1
>
> Closed at 4 a.m. You're too late.

> JAMES
>
> It's 4:01. Are you serious? My flight to
> New York is at 7.

> AIRPORT MAN 1
>
> I'm deadly serious. We take one
> minute very seriously here at British
> Airways.

ENTITLED RAGE, a portly Indian businessman with gorgeous
hair, begins walking in tight circles behind JAMES and
huffing and puffing.

> ENTITLED RAGE
>
> Perfect! Absolutely fucking PERFECT!
> FUCK! SHIT! AAAAAARRGH! CUNT!
> FUCKING CUNT!

JAMES turns around in horror to view ENTITLED RAGE,
flailing about in a tizzy.

CENTER CENTER

AIRPORT MAN 1

Sir, if you can't calm down, I'll have to
call security.

To JAMES:

You'll have to speak with the help desk
in order to rebook.

*He points to adjacent help desk. JAMES gathers his two
large suitcases and walks over to it, face dark.*

JAMES

Hi. I need to rebook my flight to New
York City as soon as possible. I've got
a very important campaign shoot for
American Ballet Theatre's *Eightieth
Anniversary* brochure. You see, I'm a
principal dancer and am therefore very
important. Hundreds of elderly people
will be wondering where my picture is
when they receive their brochures in the
mail. Old people go absolutely mad for
the mail. I mustn't miss that shoot! The
elderly need me!

*Sirens blare and the lights shift. JAMES launches into
opening musical number, a check-in desk rendition of "When
I Grow Up" by the Pussycat Dolls.*

STRANDED IN CASABLANCA

                    AIRPORT LADY 1
OK. You've come to the right place.
I'm your lady! You're in luck! Gee whiz,
are you in the right place at the
right time!

JAMES hands her his US passport.

Well, as you've booked through a third
party, we won't be able to waive the
flight-change fee, and you'll need to
pay full price for a new ticket. Aaaand
it's Thanksgiving weekend and there
aren't any direct flights to New York
City for a full week. If you want to get
back, you'll have to do multiple
connecting flights. Is that all right?

*CRYING GIRL begins moaning behind JAMES in line. She is a
petite woman in her mid-twenties with a tear-streaked face
that displays unbelievable tragedy. She is speaking on her
mobile phone.*

                    CRYING GIRL
Daddy, it's insane here! Everyone's
insane! They wouldn't even let me check
in! Can you believe it?! I'm at the help
desk, which should actually be called
the FUCKING BITCH DESK!

CRYING GIRL begins to weep uncontrollably.

JAMES

OK. What are my options?

AIPORT LADY 1

Well, let's see. You've come to the right
place. I'll get you set up. Might even
be a better flight!

*Her fingers clack cheerfully on her keyboard while she looks
up periodically to perform a manic, saccharine smile
at JAMES.*

Here's one! And check-in ends in an
hour, so that's perfect!

Frowns at her screen.

Oop! It's gone. Better act quickly if
we're going to save the old people of
New York City! OK, here's another one!
But it's $47,000. Will that do?

JAMES

Wincing:

It's a bit high. Anything cheaper?

AIRPORT LADY 1

Let's you and me have a look-see. Ah,
yes. Fancy going through Japan? Hmm,
probably not. Ah, OK. Here's the one!

I've got you going from London to
Casablanca to Boston to New York for
$1,600 on Royal Air Maroc. We must act
fast! There are a lot of weeping twenty-
somethings with daddy's credit card in
line behind you.

                    JAMES
Yes, OK. I'll try to get a refund for
the other flight.

Hands AIRPORT LADY 1 his credit card.

                AIRPORT LADY 1
Excellent. Aaaaaaaand you're all set.
Here's your boarding pass and you can
check in back where you tried and failed
before. Thank you for choosing Gatwick
Airport and do try to be here
approximately thirty hours in advance
next time.

JAMES walks to the check-in desk.

                AIRPORT MAN 1
Ah, back so soon?

JAMES hands AIRPORT MAN 1 his passport and boarding pass.

Two bags? OK, that'll be $300. Let's
just make sure they're under seven
pounds each.

JAMES hoists them up onto the scale one at a time.

> Sorry, sunshine, but they're both
> overweight. Too fat. Chubby. Chunky.
> Corpulent. That'll be $900 extra per bag.

JAMES hands AIRPORT MAN 1 his credit card begrudgingly.

Blackout.

Scene Two

AT ROYAL AIR MAROC GATE. 5 A.M.

JAMES texts his boyfriend, Dan, back in New York City.

> JAMES'S IPHONE
> They wouldn't let me check in. I'm
> literally going to explode. Everything
> was sold out because of fucking
> Thanksgiving. Now I have to fly to
> Boston via Mofuckingrocco. It's 5 a.m.
> and my flight is at 11 a.m. I have six
> hours to wait. I am very depressed and
> my funds are depleted. And I'm still
> drunk.

JAMES looks around at the gate and sees ENTITLED RAGE and CRYING GIRL sitting across from him. ENTITLED RAGE is snoring loudly and CRYING GIRL is on the phone again.

CRYING GIRL

OMG. I can't even. Can you even? I mean,
can anyone even?! The man at the desk
literally was a dog. Like full dog.
Ugh, he was legit barking. I was like,
"Can I check in?" and he was all,
"BOW WOW! WOOF! NO!" Ugh! I'm never
leaving the States again. London is
full of poison dog people! I am so
fucking mad at Jassica for taking
the later flight. I begged her to
fly with me and she was all, "That's
too early. No way, Jose!" Serves
me right for having a friend named
Jassica.

Blackout.

AT ROYAL AIR MAROC GATE. 9 A.M.

*More travelers have arrived and are sitting, scattered
about. There's a morning airport din.*

GATE AGENT 1

Over gate intercom:

Chipper cheerio, travelers! Uh-oh,
SpaghettiOs, I've got some bad news.
Your last-resort flight to Dubai or
Chechnya or whatever . . . oh,

Casablanca, is now delayed by thirty
minutes. We're sorry-not-sorry for the
inconvenience.

*GATE AGENT 1 clicks the receiver down and CRYING GIRL
begins a soft whimpering. ENTITLED RAGE perks up.*

ENTITLED RAGE
What?!?! Ahhh, absolutely not! Of course
it's delayed! Satan invented air travel!

JAMES'S IPHONE
Hey, babe. My flight to Morocco is now
delayed. I'm worried I won't make my
connection. I don't know what to do. I
really don't want to be stranded in
Casablanca.

DAN'S IPHONE
I'm sorry. Take a couple deep breaths,
my love. I dunno if it's the right time,
but here's the Pussycat Dolls'
performance from the other day!

JAMES'S IPHONE
It's always the right time for the
Pussycat Dolls.

*JAMES watches "React" by the Pussycat Dolls on his phone.
The airport scene darkens, and five spotlights appear on
five passengers, including ENTITLED RAGE and CRYING GIRL. In*

*a scene of pure fantasy, they perform the song as the
Pussycat Dolls.*

>   And we got a tilt at the end! I was
>   waiting for it!

>   DAN'S IPHONE
>   Same. Haha. Also, her little vagina
>   covering!

>   GATE AGENT 1

Over gate intercom:

>   Hello, happy travelers! Betcha wanna
>   know what's the 4-1-1. What's the sitch.
>   The scoop. The tea. Welp, looks like
>   we've got another delay c-c-comin'
>   your way. Let's tack on another thirty
>   minutes to our already delayed
>   flight. That's right, an hour total
>   delay! Yay!

GATE AGENT 1 clicks off intercom.

>   ENTITLED RAGE
>   This is insane. Who do I need to speak
>   to? I'm so busy and important it's crazy!

Blackout.

Scene Three

ROYAL AIR MAROC AIRPLANE INTERIOR. 12 P.M.

All passengers are seated, their bags stowed in the overhead bins.

> JAMES'S IPHONE
> The cabin crew has been told to identify
> the owner of each bag in the overhead
> bins. They're going through every bag
> trying to find one passenger who might
> have brought a bag aboard and then left
> the plane! So strange. Kind of scary.

The flight attendants move from row to row, inspecting each bag in the overhead bins and asking the passengers to whom each bag belongs.

> There's a beautiful Moroccan flight
> attendant tho. So tall. Unibrow. Should
> be a model.

> DAN'S IPHONE
> Hot. Sleep with him.

> ENTITLED RAGE

Stands up from his seat in front of JAMES.

> What's going on?! Why the hell did we go
> through security if you're just gonna do

it all over again on the plane? C'mon!
I'm gonna get stuck in Morocco! I'm
gonna miss my connection! Fucking hell!
Then what?! Hey! Listen up! Anybody else
on their way to Boston?

*Many other passengers raise their hands or turn around to
nod at ENTITLED RAGE.*

What the hell are we gonna do?! SHIT!

UNIBROW
Sir, please sit down! We are about to
begin taxiing.

*UNIBROW is clearly annoyed. He scoffs and rolls his eyes
like a teenager.*

We'll stop inspecting the bags and make
everyone wait until you sit down.

ENTITLED RAGE takes his seat forcefully.

*UNIBROW mutters to his colleague, a short woman with bright-
red-dyed hair.*

I hate this fucking bullshit.

*The cabin lights flicker and shift to a hazy glow. UNIBROW
begins singing the Pussycat Dolls' "I Hate This Part," as
CRYING GIRL continues whimpering and ENTITLED RAGE fidgets
and grumbles in his seat. UNIBROW continues slowly checking*

each tiny bag, with the assistance of his portly peer, until
the song finishes and they are finally ready for takeoff.

PILOT

Over intercom.

Flight attendants, please be seated for
departure.

ENTITLED RAGE

Ugh! FINALLY!

Blackout.

ACT TWO

Scene One

CASABLANCA AIRPORT. ROYAL AIR MAROC ARRIVAL GATE.
2:15 P.M.

JAMES'S IPHONE

Landed in Casablanca!
Just got a text that my flight from
Boston to New York City has been
canceled.
Cool cool.
There's no way I'm making my connection.
It's in 10 minutes.

I asked if I could deplane first and
they were like, "fuck u bitch."
I sat next to the most annoying person
ever. Her elbow was halfway in my lap and
she didn't understand the seatbelt. She
made me do it up for her multiple times.

DAN'S IPHONE
Fucking lunatic.

JAMES, ENTITLED RAGE, CRYING GIRL, and the rest of the
passengers exit the plane in a rush.

ENTITLED RAGE
Are they gonna wait for us?! They HAVE
to wait for us!!

GATE AGENT 2
Oh, absolutely. They're going to wait for
each and every one of you. You had
better hurry, though. See that plane
next door? That's your plane. You had
better hurry over to the gate. Thank
goodness it's so close.

About ten people begin running to the new gate for their
connection to Boston, Massachusetts, USA.

ENTITLED RAGE
What the fuck was that lady talking
about?! Our gate is at the other end of
the airport!!

CENTER CENTER

CRYING GIRL

Oh, my god! Daddy is gonna kill me if I
miss this flight!

*CRYING GIRL is running and weeping loudly, moaning and
sniffling.*

JAMES

Which way?!

ENTITLED RAGE

That way! Let's GO!

*The travelers run in place as lights shift and pass by them
quickly to signify passage through space to the other end
of the terminal.*

*MISS AIRPLANE can be seen shuffling in the distance.
MISS AIRPLANE is a woman in a boxy, unflattering Royal
Air Maroc airplane costume. Her costume is an actual
replica of the airplane. She can be seen shuffling away
from the gate.*

**CASABLANCA AIRPORT. ROYAL AIR MAROC DEPARTURE GATE.
2:30 P.M.**

*All travelers perform exciting choreography as ENTITLED
RAGE and MISS AIRPLANE begin a sassy duet to the Pussycat
Dolls' "Wait a Minute."*

*The musical interlude concludes as the travelers finally
reach the gate.*

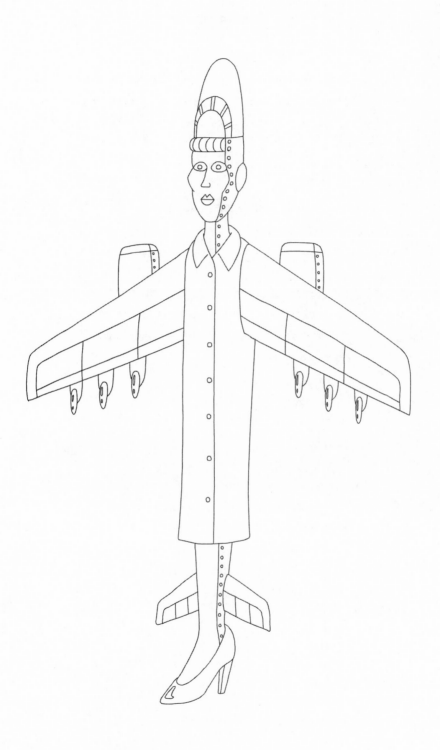

CENTER CENTER

CRYING GIRL

WAIT! Noooooooo! Oh, my god, nuh-uh! I can
like fucking still see the plane. Like it's
right there. Like I can *see* you. Ahhhhhh.

Weeps and whines. Falls to knees.

ENTITLED RAGE

Screaming and truly beside himself.

STOP THE PLANE! TURN IT AROUND! I SWEAR
TO FUCKING GOD TURN IT AROUND RIGHT NOW!
THERE'S TEN OF US, FOR GOD'S SAKE! HAVE
YOU ANY HUMANITY?!

GATE AGENT 3

Calm and quiet:

Sir, I'm sorry I can't call a plane back
once it's departed the gate. There's
nothing I can do. I'm sorry.

CRYING GIRL

I'm gonna dieeeeeeeeeeeeee!

JAMES

To GATE AGENT 3:

Now what? What do we do?

GATE AGENT 3

Well, you'll have to rebook at the
Royal Air Maroc help desk, right over
there.

Points to a long desk adjacent to the gate.

ENTITLED RAGE

Screaming:

Arrrrrrrghhhhhhhhhhhhhh!!!!!!!!!!!

GATE AGENT 3

Sir. I'm calling security.

ENTITLED RAGE

CALL YOUR FUCKING MOM FOR ALL I CARE!

*ENTITLED RAGE storms away to the help desk. The rest of the
passengers follow.*

Blackout.

Scene Two

**CASABLANCA AIRPORT. ROYAL AIR MAROC HELP DESK.
2:30 P.M.**

ENTITLED RAGE

You there. Hey!

                    HELP DESK AGENT 1
How may I help you, sir?

                      ENTITLED RAGE
Our flight just left without us. We need
to rebook.

                    HELP DESK AGENT 1
OK. Well, that was the last flight to
the United States today. We'll have to
rebook for tomorrow.

                      ENTITLED RAGE
What the FUCK?!

                       CRYING GIRL
Excayuuse me, sir. We—like, all of
us—need to get back to the United
States today. Can you make that
happen?

CRYING GIRL gestures to the whole group, which consists of:
ENTITLED RAGE, SWEATY WHITE GUY, QUIET LADY, OLD COUPLE,
BRITISH TWINS, PREPPY, AND JAMES. The whole group begins
shouting, "Yeah!" and jostling each other in a clump, trying
to get to the front of the line.

                      BRITISH TWIN 1
OY! Now you listen up, mate! Oim talkin'
to you! If you fink me 'n moy sister are
shackin' up in Casablanca fen you've got
anuva fing comin'!

                             172

                    BRITISH TWIN 2
That's roight! Moy sister could sock
you into next week, bruv! Don't let's be
a cunt!

                    BRITISH TWIN 1
Don't be a cunt!

                    QUIET LADY

Whispering:

    I've got to get home to go to work.

                  SWEATY WHITE GUY
    Yeah, me too! Gee whiz! Jiminy Cricket,
    it's hot in here! Y'all got any AC in
    this joint? Sheesh! Gadzooks!

Begins fanning himself with his passport. QUIET LADY looks
from him to BRITISH TWINS with silent derision.

PREPPY, a tall, quite handsome gentleman in business-casual
attire, steps forward to the front of the line.

                      PREPPY
    OK, everyone. Stay calm. Sir, as you can
    see, we're all here because we've missed
    our connecting flight due to delays.
    We are in dire need of getting to
    Boston. What is the best way to achieve
    our goal?

                        173

HELP DESK AGENT 1

I'm sorry, but there aren't anymore
flights today. We'll provide you with a
hotel room for the night and get you
rebooked on a flight tomorrow.

ENTITLED RAGE

NO! YOU CALL THAT PLANE BACK THIS
INSTANT, GODDAMN IT!

BRITISH TWIN 1

That's roight! Call it back roight now!

HELP DESK AGENT 1

OK. Let me go speak to my colleague.
Please wait.

*HELP DESK AGENT 1 stands up from behind the desk, puts on
his coat, grabs his folio, and walks away slowly,
disappearing into the exit doors.*

PREPPY

I'm pretty sure he just left.

CRYING GIRL

Wait . . . what?!

She begins moaning and sighing.

SWEATY WHITE GUY

Impossible. Wait, where is everyone?

PREPPY

I don't know. It's weird. The airport is
completely empty.

ENTITLED RAGE

What the fuck is this?! The Moroccan
Twilight Zone? Where did he go?!

BRITISH TWIN 2

Oi fink he up and left! Wivout a word!
That twat was very rude!

BRITISH TWIN 1

Rudest bitch eva.

SWEATY WHITE GUY

Wowzers. Quite the vocabulary. I'm going
to go look around.

*SWEATY WHITE GUY dashes down the hallway, his shirt soaked
through with sweat except for two spots surrounding his
large nipples.*

JAMES'S IPHONE

*Sends a photo to DAN'S IPHONE of a long help desk,
completely devoid of agents.*

The help desk is lit.
So many people working.
Lol.

We're all just milking around shouting,
"DOES ANYONE WORK HERE?!"

DAN'S IPHONE

Milking?

JAMES'S IPHONE

Sorry, typo. There are some amazing
characters here.
People were getting violent.
I wanna write about it.

Blackout.

CASABLANCA AIRPORT. ROYAL AIR MAROC HELP DESK. 3 P.M.

*A woman in a Royal Air Maroc uniform enters and makes her
way to a chair behind the help desk.*

QUIET LADY

Whispers:

Do you work here?

CRYING GIRL

Are you like gonna help us? Do
I live here now? Is this
my life?

(Life *pronounced luh-ee-yif-uh)*

HELP DESK AGENT 2

Yes, I'm here to help. My name is HELP
DESK AGENT 2 and I'm amazing. I'm your
savior and basically Moroccan lady
Jesus.

ENTITLED RAGE

Throws hands up and gazes to the sky.

Praise HELP DESK AGENT 2!

HELP DESK AGENT 2

My benevolence shall require each of
your passports. My goodness knows no
bounds.

Each passenger hands over their passport.

*SWEATY WHITE GUY returns from his airport sojourn. He is
completely soaked through.*

BRITISH TWIN 1

Did you go outsoide, bruv? Izzit
raining?

SWEATY WHITE GUY

Who's that?

CRYING GIRL

It's our guardian angel! She's going to
help us! Her name, should you like,

deign to utter it, is HELP DESK
AGENT 2.

                    SWEATY WHITE GUY
Huzzah!

Hands over his passport.

                    HELP DESK AGENT 2
OK, listen up, disciples. I'm going to
rebook you on a flight tomorrow at 4
p.m. to New York City and from there to
Boston. No more bellyaching because this
is the ONLY option. You want to get home
alive? Then listen to me. You're going
to exit without your bags. They'll be
loaded onto your flight tomorrow
automatically. You're gonna get on a
shuttle bus and go to a hotel. A shuttle
will pick you up in the morning to bring
you back here. I'm all you've ever
needed. Praise me.

                    ALL

In unison:

Praise HELP DESK AGENT 2!

Blackout.

ACT THREE

Scene 1

CASABLANCA ROACH MOTEL. CHECK-IN DESK. 5 P.M.

The travelers enter the motel looking bedraggled and carsick. They either have only their carry-on luggage or no bags at all. They are greeted by a chipper, cheerful man at the check-in desk.

> ROACH MOTEL CONCIERGE
>
> WELCOME TO THE CASABLANCA ROACH MOTEL!
> You are lucky to be here. Better than
> sleeping on floor of airport, no?
> Important information: there is bar.
> That's it . . . hahahahaha!

> CRYING GIRL
>
> But like, where are our rooms-uh? I'm so
> tired-uh.

> ROACH MOTEL CONCIERGE
>
> I've got your keys here. One for each of
> you . . . unless any of you are sleeping
> together. Hahahahaha! Now listen, there
> is bar. You need good drink and foods
> before going to rooms. We have pasta
> without sauce and bread from last year.
> Very delicious.

ROACH MOTEL CONCIERGE gestures across the hall to the bar, where a bartender is brandishing a loaf of dry bread in one hand and a bottle of whiskey in the other. She accidentally drops the bread and it makes a loud thud! *and lodges itself into the linoleum floor.*

Blackout.

Scene 2

CASABLANCA ROACH MOTEL BAR. 7 P.M.

PREPPY is standing at the high bar with ENTITLED RAGE as JAMES groggily approaches.

JAMES

Hey. I almost fell asleep, but then
realized I wasn't drunk yet.

PREPPY & ENTITLED RAGE

In unison:

Same.

JAMES

To bartender:

A Jameson on the rocks, please.

ROACH MOTEL BARTENDER is a mime. She emphatically gestures and does open-mouth smiles a lot. She pours JAMES his beverage and he joins PREPPY and ENTITLED RAGE.

As she hands JAMES the Jameson, the travelers freeze and the lights switch to a hot pink. ROACH MOTEL BARTENDER launches into a very brief rendition of the Pussycat Dolls' "Bottle Pop."

After her number, the lights switch back like nothing ever happened. The travelers unfreeze.

> I'm JAMES. Funny how we're just getting
> to names.

>   ENTITLED RAGE
>   Hey. I'm ENTITLED RAGE.

Extends a hand to JAMES.

>   PREPPY
>   And I'm PREPPY.

Also extends a hand to JAMES. The three of them perform a cartoonish crossed-arm handshake and nod at each other.

CRYING GIRL emerges from the elevator and walks over to the bar to speak to the gentlemen.

CRYING GIRL

Umm, like the rooms are made of tile.
Like all of it is tile-uh. I couldn't go
to sleep yet.

JAMES

We just did names. I'm JAMES, that's
ENTITLED RAGE, and PREPPY.

CRYING GIRL

I'm CRYING GIRL.

ENTITLED RAGE

Want a beer? I'm getting this round.

CRYING GIRL nods and ENTITLED RAGE orders three beers, as
JAMES already has a whiskey.

CRYING GIRL

This is so crazy. I can't believe we're
stuck here. We're not even like in the
city. Did anyone look out the window?

PREPPY

Yeah, I saw the barbed wire, too.

JAMES

So, we're in prison?

CRYING GIRL

Or hell. Or both.

Whimpers quietly.

> JAMES

> So, what does everyone do for work? I'm
> a ballet dancer. I'm missing a *very*
> important campaign shoot. My face was
> gonna be on a bus!!!

> ENTITLED RAGE

> Like Carrie Bradshaw?

> JAMES

> Like Carrie Bradshaw.

> ENTITLED RAGE

> I'm a banker.

> PREPPY

> I work for a wind energy company.

> CRYING GIRL

> I go to MITeeyah. I'm gonna be an
> astrophysicist-uh.

*ROACH MOTEL BARTENDER is eavesdropping and mimes a WOW
reaction.*

> JAMES

> Where are you all from? I'm from
> Connecticut but live in New York City.
> Manhattan. I'm so busy.

ENTITLED RAGE
London. I'm also busy.

PREPPY
Yorkshire.

CRYING GIRL
Orange County. Like *The O.C.* That show
was stupid but like, everything.

She looks to JAMES.

So, you missed check-in at Gatwick, too,
right?

JAMES
By like one fucking minute!

CRYING GIRL
Same. Were you OK? You honestly looked
quite drunk.

She giggles coyly. Perhaps flirting.

JAMES
I was very drunk. All because of a
handsome Irish man. Looked a bit like you,
PREPPY. Well, this is what happened . . .

They all lean in to hear and . . .

Blackout.

Scene 3

LONDON HIPSTER NIGHTCLUB. MIDNIGHT.

*JAMES and RUPERT order a beverage at a crowded bar. RUPERT
is a handsome Irish ballet dancer, whom JAMES had met
during his week in London.*

*Disco lights swirl and flash. The club is loud and
people are having a wonderful time. Our heroes yell over
the din.*

> RUPERT

Shouting.

> WHAT DO YOU WANT?!

> JAMES
> JUST A BEER! I'M ALREADY DRUNK FROM THE
> PUB AND THE COCKTAIL BAR. THAT WAS A
> LOT OF WHISKEY! HAHA!

> RUPERT
> HAHA! COMIN' RIGHT UP!

*JAMES waits by the back wall. RUPERT shoots him a smile
over his shoulder as he gets the drinks and JAMES thinks,
"Goodness gracious, he's handsome."*

*RUPERT does a silly jig over to JAMES, sloshing the drinks
over his hands and laughing.*

RUPERT

So, what are we doing here?

JAMES

Huh?

RUPERT

You know what I mean.

JAMES

Hehe. Well, I think I know what you mean.

RUPERT

Don't you have a boyfriend?

JAMES

Yeah, I do. For twelve years. We're in an open relationship. You have a boyfriend, too, don't you?

RUPERT

RUPERT steps closer to JAMES.

Well, yes. He's away right now for work. I don't know what I'm doing here with you. We're not open. I couldn't resist.

JAMES steps closer to RUPERT.

JAMES

Do you want to dance with me?

RUPERT

What?

JAMES

Yelling over the noise:

DO YOU. WANT TO. DANCE WITH ME?

RUPERT

Yelling over the noise:

I ABSOLUTELY WANT TO DANCE WITH YOU!

JAMES takes RUPERT'S hand and leads him to the crowded dance floor.

The crowd parts to admit our heroes. The lights change and an enormous disco ball lowers from the ceiling. A monster of a dance number ensues to a mashup of the Pussycat Dolls' "Don't Cha" and "Buttons." JAMES and RUPERT take turns singing along in a sexy, "we should/we shouldn't" dance battle. Major choreography is performed by the other clubgoers.

As the song ends, our heroes meet in the center of the floor, under the disco ball. All goes quiet as they lean into each other, their foreheads touching and their hands clasping. Their lips almost meet . . . and . . .

Blackout.

Scene 4

CASABLANCA ROACH MOTEL BAR. 8 P.M.

*Lights up and we see the travelers engrossed in JAMES'S
story.*

> CRYING GIRL
>
> Then what?!

> PREPPY
>
> Did you kiss hi—

> ENTITLED RAGE

Interrupting:

> FUCKING HELL! JUST TELL US WHAT
> HAPPENED!!!

> JAMES
>
> No.

*The travelers settle back into their barstools, clearly
disappointed.*

> I didn't want to interfere with his
> relationship, so I called a taxi and he
> insisted on seeing me home. I was
> convinced he'd come up with me, but he
> didn't. I got out of the taxi, he rolled

down the window, I bent down and took
his face in my hands and kissed him on
the cheek. It was lightly raining and
Bermondsey stood stock still in the
night. Without a word, I disappeared
into my hotel and that was that.

CRYING GIRL
So *that's* why you were drunk at 4 a.m.
at Gatwick Airport.

JAMES
Correct. Speaking of which, I need
another. I'll get this round.

*JAMES gestures to the bartender for another round of
drinks. The lights shift, the travelers freeze, and the
bartender launches into another short rendition of the
Pussycat Dolls' "Bottle Pop."*

*The lights shift back and the travelers unfreeze, one round
of drinks richer. JAMES hands out the beverages as a short,
stout, rough-looking man enters the bar.*

*PORTUGUESE SEAMAN is a forty-something ship inspector from
Portugal.*

PORTUGUESE SEAMAN
Hello, barkeep. I'll have a pint
of whatever piss you're serving
tonight. Ha!

He looks at the travelers.

What's going on here? Are you airport
people? Stranded in Casablanca?

*He and the travelers look sharply to the fourth wall with
sardonic smiles.*

PREPPY

Yep. Stuck here till tomorrow.

PORTUGUESE SEAMAN

Lucky you found me! Casablanca ain't all
that bad. It's good for two things . . .
bars and bitches. Ha!

The travelers all roll their eyes.

PORTUGUESE SEAMAN looks at CRYING GIRL.

Hello, sad beauty. My name is PORTUGUESE
SEAMAN. Once you get a taste of
PORTUGUESE SEAMAN, you'll be begging for
more. You'll be wishing you had
PORTUGUESE SEAMAN all over you.

*CRYING GIRL makes a big show of being sick and vomiting all
over the floor. The other travelers all join in, taking
turns clutching their stomachs and retching. They laugh.*

You'd like to know more about me, no?
I'm a ship inspector. I've been here for

a week without work. The vessel is
delayed, so I'm delayed at my next port.
You can't deliver PORTUGUESE SEAMAN
without a vessel. Ha!

The travelers ignore him.

Well, I have been having a good time
here. Even though the vessel is not yet
here. I can't wait to see the vessel.
It's going to be a big vessel. A
marvelous vessel. The vessel.

CRYING GIRL

Can you not?

PORTUGUESE SEAMAN

All right, sad beauty. For you, I will
do anything. I will lay down my enormous
vessel before you and hope that you will
board it. You can ride it till you meet
your next dock. Ha!

ENTITLED RAGE

OK, you twat. Listen up. We have all had
a fucking fuckity fuck of a travel day.
We're just trying to have a drink and do
some depression bonding, so SHUT . . .
THE FUCK . . . UP!!!

Blackout.

CENTER CENTER

A spotlight appears on CRYING GIRL's face. She launches into the Dave Audé disco remix of the Pussycat Dolls' "Hush Hush; Hush Hush" with the other travelers as her backup Dolls. She sings the song and dances aggressively at PORTUGUESE SEAMAN. The song finishes with the whole group kicking PORTUGUESE SEAMAN out of the bar.

Lights shift back to the bar and the travelers are laughing and when they stop, the BARTENDER is still silently laughing hysterically.

> JAMES

OK, it's my bedtime.

> CRYING GIRL

Yeah, me too. I'm so tired-uh. We've got
an early flight tomorrow.

JAMES gets up and pays the tab.

> PREPPY

Hopefully no hitches tomorrow.

> ENTITLED RAGE

I don't think I could take it.

> JAMES

I don't think you could either.

JAMES chuckles and starts walking toward the elevator. He stops and turns around to address the others.

It was nice meeting you all. This was a
wild and horrible travel day, but I'm
glad we went through it together. It
just goes to show . . . you can suffer
anything with the right group of people.
So, thanks.

*He smiles, turns around, and pushes the button to call the
elevator. The elevator dings and the doors open. It's
chock-full of all the travelers from the hellacious day,
plus the agents and clerks they'd encountered along the way:
CONCIERGE, BARTENDER, BRITISH TWINS, QUIET LADY, SWEATY
WHITE GUY, OLD COUPLE, and PORTUGUESE SEAMAN. They pour out
of the doors and . . .*

*the lights bump up and a finale begins. BRITISH TWINS
1 AND 2 step forward slowly, with benevolent smiles on
their faces, and begin singing the Pussycat Dolls'
"Stickwitu."*

*The entire cast sings along, in a lovey-dovey, grab-a-
shoulder-and-sway type of affair.*

"Nobody ever made me feel this way. I'ma
stick wit u."

Blackout.

*Bows and curtain calls are executed to a mashup reprise of
"I Will Survive" and "Hush Hush; Hush Hush" as the company
receives the accolades they so deserve. Tears stream down*

the midwestern tourists' faces as they revel in the joy of an obstacle triumphed over. They sing along and clap to the iconic musical stylings of the Pussycat Dolls.

                    VOICE OF GOD
          Thus, a Broadway smash is born. A travel
          nightmare turned friendship musical
          featuring the extensive and relatable
          catalog of the United States' most
          prized artists, the Pussycat Dolls.

                    THE END.

LOATHE, REVILE, ABHOR, DETEST!

While my opinion may be divisive, I find ballet to be the most undeniably athletic form of dance. It's just as physically difficult as elite sports, but presents additional challenges. Imagine if a weightlifter or a tennis player were asked to perform their tasks without betraying the difficulty of their movements. Now, I'd like you to ask those athletes to tell a story about human emotions and experiences with intuitive and expressive musicality. I'd like you to ensure that their bodies fit into a narrow range of acceptable dimensions. *That's* what a ballet dancer is. An elite athlete, an expressive actor, and a visual representation of music itself, all at once.

Because of its rigid physical requirements, ballet has a way of making one obsess over every little detail of one's appearance. While a normie might say, "I wish my breasts were the same size," a ballet dancer would say, "I wish my kneecaps were rotated three more degrees outward and made of flawless diamonds." Physical minutiae become obsessions. Ballet, more than any other art form, is reliant on physical features we cannot change. Our genetics—bone structure, height, weight, and proportions—either dictate or sabotage our success.

BEFORE I KNEW what dancing was, I loved dancing. My mother had a hilarious collection of workout VHS tapes that I never saw her do: *Jazzercise, Buns of Steel,* and *Jane Fonda's Workout.* Jane Fonda was my babysitter, my first dance teacher, and perhaps even my mother. I loved the music and the movement, not to mention Jane's obvious beauty. I recognized what a goddess she was at the age of six. Every day, I'd pop in a Jane Fonda workout tape and grab a chair to do step-ups onto. I'd dance along to the eighties soundtrack and giggle as I wiggled. As a result, I was strangely muscular. My siblings would show me off to their teenage friends and say, "My six-year-old brother has an eight-pack!"

At nine, I started taking dance classes at my local studio in Fairfield, Connecticut. Jazz class was my favorite. It was hugely energetic. I'd bop along to the era's hit music, doing kicks and splits in my jazz boots. Ballet, on the other hand, was my absolute nemesis. Our studio didn't have a pianist, so our music came from cassette tapes. To go from Prince to canned piano music was very difficult for me.

In ballet class, the boys were made to wear white cap-sleeved leotards and black tights, with white ballet shoes and socks. I recall looking at myself in the stretched-mylar mirrors. "Is that E.T.?" I asked myself. My arms were too gangly. My rib cage was enormous. My kneecaps stuck out at right angles. My shoulders were slumped for-

ward. And my face was completely asymmetrical. The bones on one side of my face grew much faster than those on the other, so it looked as though I had a jawbreaker in one of my cheeks at all times, and my teeth were rotated at impossible angles. My father spent much of his limited cash trying to prevent me from having a catastrophic, crooked underbite that would erode my jaw joints. I spent nearly a decade in braces, palate expanders, and headgear. Each night, I'd get ready for bed and install upon my head a device so horrific that even medieval torturers would have shied away from it. Its wires threaded into wire-plated nooses that affixed to my rearmost molars. I'd then bite down on a plastic-molded guard that reimagined where my teeth were supposed to fit. Rubber bands were fastened to large wire protuberances that stuck out from the mouthpiece and connected to a cradle that wrapped all the way around my head, effectively yanking my entire jaw to the weaker side in an effort to retrain my bones. I am grateful for that torture device, even though it was an absolute nightmare. Without it, my chin might have rested on my right shoulder and my face might've resembled a crescent moon.

I recall taking a private ballet lesson when I was ten years old. I had arrived at the lesson wearing my black tights and a T-shirt so enormous it ended below my knees. My teacher, Karen, asked me to remove it. I obliged reluctantly. I have a small mole under my left armpit, and at the time, I thought it to be a repulsive mutation. My self-consciousness was so extreme that throughout the whole class, I kept my arm clamped tightly to my rib cage, so as not to reveal my mole to my teacher. I was trying to execute a simple *tombé, pas de bourrée, glissade, saut de chat* combination with one arm glued to my side when my teacher said, "STOP! WHAT ON EARTH ARE YOU DOING WITH YOUR ARMS?!" No one had told me that my mole was hideous; I had decided it all on my own. I figured that anything that made me a little different was undesirable.

But it wasn't until I went away to ballet school at Virginia School of the Arts that I was confronted by what is known as the "ballet body." Despite having spent the two previous summers at American Ballet Theatre's Summer Intensive, I had thus far remained fairly ignorant about all the exacting specifications that seemed to be prerequisites for a successful career in ballet. In Virginia, I heard comments like "I wish my knees were hyperextended like Mary's," "He has a lovely, short torso," and "Look at those long toes!" over and over again. I was bewildered. I thought, "Isn't there just fat and skinny, short and tall?" No, little James, no.

If you're wondering "What in the actual fuck is he going on about?" here's a crash course in the Male Ballet Body. Highly arched feet with flexible ankles and strong toes. Slender ankles and knee joints. Preposterously long, hyperextended legs. Open, turned-out hips. Long muscles. Slim waist, broad shoulders. Long arms with expressive hands and fingers. A long neck and a beautiful face. This is a farce, if you ask me. Ballet requires extreme fitness, so if there's a body that's fit, it's fit to do ballet. I don't believe it's about being fat or thin, I believe it's about having the strength and endurance to survive the difficulty of professional classical ballet.

With that said, in my youth, I became increasingly aware of the way my rib cage was shaped, the way my knees were shaped, my shoulders, my feet, my hips, my neck, and more. I started feeling shame about my lack of hyperextension, my just-OK feet, and my strangely shaped skeletal frame. I'd look at the other students with jealous eyes. Reading *Dance Magazine*, I'd be confronted by ballet mutants like David Hallberg and Vladimir Malakhov, whose bodies are made of actual spaghetti. Why should *they* have the perfect ballet body? I began to resent my genetics, which is absolutely insane.

This feeling followed me, and even worsened, as I began my professional career. As an apprentice in Boston Ballet II, I was surrounded by excellent dancers with finely honed physiques. My then-boyfriend, Mason, had wildly hyperextended knees and arched feet. His hips flopped open to produce the desired turnout effect. I'd stare at my knees in the mirror and shoot hateful daggers at myself. I kept working, identifying areas where I needed to improve. I'd watch the dancers who were more proficient than me and try to analyze why. But ballet class after ballet class, I'd still gaze upon my ironing-board, inflexible arabesque with tearful rage.

FINALLY, a vital change happened. A *revelation*. I began to notice that not all the best dancers in the company had the best "ballet bodies." These ideal bodies, which students like myself had obsessed over for ages, didn't guarantee you talent or intelligence. Talent without intelligence is like spaghetti without a plate: a mess. My brain was the key to becoming a better dancer.

I started working differently in class, trying to make up for the things I supposedly lacked. I used what hip turnout I actually had to create the illusion of even greater turnout. I found that even without "perfectly arched feet" I could be as expressive with my little hooves as I could with my hands and fingers. I looked at my knees not as bent, knobbly branches, but as tools to draw attention to where I wanted it drawn. I concentrated on true and proper classical ballet technique, without obsessing over inhuman details. I began using my muscles properly instead of just wrenching my body this way and that. I immediately felt more in control of my body and my dancing became less accidental. This new focus gave me the freedom to dance with more technical precision and artistry.

I look back on the time I spent hating myself bitterly. I eventually learned that denial prevents growth. I needed to just get over it to truly become myself. And when I see that people get stuck on the perfect "ballet body," nothing can change for them, because they themselves can't change until they want to. I'm not talking about their bodies, but their minds.

I've adapted RuPaul's famous line to better suit my needs: "If you can't love *your* ballet body, how in the hell you gonna love somebody else's ballet body?"

THE TENANT:
A NEAR-DEATH EXPERIENCE

In 2017, it was about time for me to have a midcareer crisis. I could get only so far dancing all the lead roles in ABT's rep, right?

Principal dancers in large ballet companies such as ABT have an egocentric duty to pursue projects outside the realm of their typical seasons. Such projects are commonly known as vanity projects, as they tend to be vainer than Carly Simon karaoke. Two years earlier I had participated as a dancer in my fellow ABT principal Daniil Simkin's vanity project, aptly named *Intensio*. It was a harrowing and seemingly endless process that yielded a somewhat entertaining show with wonderful dancers who happened to be some of my best friends. Daniil is a savvy and curious artist; I've learned a lot from him.

These vanity projects are often housed at the Joyce Theater, a small venue nestled in the heart of one of Manhattan's many gayborhoods: Chelsea. The Joyce provides ballet's stars a place to writhe around to the spoken word, framed by Windows 95 screen savers; one can also go there to see dance styles ranging from classical ballet to fifteenth-century penis puppetry. To the left of the building, one might shop for dildos the size of a Renaissance fair turkey leg, and to the right, one might stop in for a coffee at a Starbucks populated predominantly by homosexual hobos. There's a quote on the Joyce's brick exterior by the eccentric and prolific choreographer Twyla Tharp: "Art is the only way to run away without leaving home." This is ironic, for the sole reason that one must leave one's home to go to a theater to watch the damn dance. Quotes are tough in that way: they look great on the side of a building, but they rarely make sense.

I know the Joyce sounds atrocious, but it's actually an important and exciting theater. It seems to be run by the fearless, who are wont to give artists a safe space to get freaky without fear of divine retribution. And after four years of dancing roles like Prince Albrecht, Prince Siegfried, Prince Désiré, et cetera with ABT, I was ready to get freaky.

I had contacts from my time dancing *Intensio* at the Joyce still in my Rolodex, so I sent them a meek inquiry asking if I could do a show. They agreed to meet with me at Le Pain Quotidien, a restaurant I've nicknamed "the Bread Quotient," as I find Le Pain Quotidien an offensively pretentious name for something so mediocre. Naturally, I was incredibly excited about the meeting and composed a simulacrum of a PowerPoint presentation for a show I'd dreamed up titled *Manhattan*—a one-act murder-mystery dance show scored with classic jazz tunes sung by the greats. Over a boiled egg and tasteless bread that would have made Denmark proud, the Joyce Theater higher-ups patiently suffered my delusional musings and said they would think about it. Then they asked me if I'd ever met the British choreographer and director Arthur Pita. They thought we'd get along swimmingly.

———

WEEKS LATER, the Joyce Theater arranged for me to meet Arthur. Arthur is a very sunny Portuguese/South African/British man who stands around five foot ten, with jet-black hair, an olive complexion, glasses that rest low on his nose, and a full and dark mustache that rests complacently on his top teeth, which are almost always showing in a decidedly British way. His clothing is a mixture of Muji utilitarian and chav tracksuits, and he almost never wears shoes, opting instead to shuffle about in cotton socks. His confidence allows you to admire him without hesitation, and his congenial sense of humor makes him immediately one of your favorite people. And thankfully, he's attractive without being somebody that I'm worried I'll want to sleep with. It's important not to shit where one eats.

"Have you heard of the novel *The Tenant*?" Arthur asked me.

I hadn't.

"Have you seen the film?"

I hadn't.

"Well, you should read it. I think you'd make an excellent Trelkovsky."

Arthur fascinated me, and I desperately wanted to know more, so I excitedly read *The Tenant* in a few short days. Arthur was right: Monsieur Trelkovsky—the story's protagonist, if one may call him that—was mine.

It's hard to explain the events in *The Tenant*, a 1964 novel by Roland Topor, as they're up for much interpretation. An inoffensive summary is that a Parisian of Polish descent named Trelkovsky is possessed by the spirit of the former tenant of his apartment, Miss Simone Choule, who launched herself out her window in an apparent suicide attempt. Trelkovsky's obsession with Simone begins with his visiting her in the hospital, where she soon dies, and continues as he discovers more and more about her by living in her apartment. The story ends with Trelkovsky transforming into Simone and launching himself not once, but twice, out the window. The final pages—I apologize, reader, for spoiling the story—consist of Trelkovsky languishing in the very same Parisian hospital where Simone died, squeaking out guttural utterances while bandaged up like a decidedly chic mummy. Horror this, horror that.

It was obvious to me that I should play Trelkovsky, what with my experiences in general weirdness and the art of drag. I called Arthur and the team at the Joyce and gave my approval, and Arthur declared the next stage in the process to be "The Workshop." This intimidated me, as I've never had the luxury of bumbling around in a studio without knowing exactly what was to be created. In the ballet companies I've danced for, one generally shows up with the knowledge of what is to be danced, and if it's a new piece of choreography, there's rarely the luxury of time to do much fiddling about. But Arthur wasn't yet sure of the build of the show. Was it a one-man show? Was it a duet? Was there a large ensemble? Was there a marching band?

A small number of people were welcomed into the workshop: myself, Arthur, his assistant Nina, my then-boyfriend Dan, and three other dancers, Calvin, Jesse, and Navarra. The majority of what we did were acting exercises, which is something I'd never done before. It's funny how ballet has remained so completely separate from other art forms, even though it contains so many elements of music, acting, and other styles of dance. So much of "ballet acting" is so unbelievable that I find it ridiculous that we haven't married true acting training to our classical ballet training. The short of it is that we often look like archaic psychopaths, tearing about the stage biting our index fingers and flailing our arms like startled chimps. Why is ballet acting separate from realist acting? How did this happen? And why are so few dancers challenging it? I believe the two can and should unite.

The Tenant has some out-there parts that we tackled quite early on. I'm assuming Arthur wanted to gauge my willingness to "go there." One of the earlier plot elements had me rubbing clementines over

Navarra's breasts in an imaginary hospital over the prone, comatose body of Jesse. Keep in mind that I had met these dancers the day before. Such is the beautiful thing about being a dancer: one can rub clementines on a stranger's breasts without feeling the least bit like the neighborhood creep. Or perhaps I've just felt like the neighborhood creep all along?

Possibly the most difficult material to tackle was the transformation into Simone. Arthur asked me to bring in a traditional woman's skirt suit, pantyhose, a wig, drugstore makeup, and a pair of heels, all of which I already owned. He set up a chair very close to the mirror and directed me to take my time changing out of my traditionally masculine clothing and into the traditionally feminine clothing. The Topor text is very rich during this scene and offered an exciting challenge. Trelkovsky's possession by Simone Choule, literal or figurative, would prove to be the most important test of the entire creative process. The easiest scene for me to grasp theatrically was the scene in which my character becomes very ill. I spent much of this workshop day feigning extreme fevers and shivering violently. I'd twitch and shudder, executing various acrobatics mixed with the morose self-pity of a person unwell.

That evening, with the "in-studio showing" (a short performance of accumulated workshop material) looming on the horizon of the following day, I actually became violently ill. Perhaps I had convinced my body that I truly *was* ill. Is that even possible? A fever spiked within me, my tonsils swelled to itchy grapefruits, and my bowels evacuated in a most uncivilized fashion. Strep throat, my arch nemesis, had struck again. I still, to this day, have my tonsils and they are as trying as fussy babies. They consistently go out of their way to enjoy infection. I'm sure it has something to do with the maniacally anxious way in which I gnaw at my fingernails.

After a few days, a round of antibiotics, and a loss of six pounds, I performed the in-studio showing. We hadn't actually come up with much movement, but we had a sketch of what the storytelling would look like. During this period, I had lightened my hair to a sickly yellowish orange, which made my skin appear jaundiced and vaguely unwell. I don't know what I was thinking, but that's a sentiment I've felt more often than not when reminiscing.

Immediately after the showing, I was subjected to a photo/video shoot for promotional materials. The Joyce wanted to make a selling package for potential sponsors of the show. My face was shaven at the time, and my cheekbones were threatening to puncture my skin and expose my skull as a result of my whirlwind illness. I had lost weight so quickly that my face appeared to be a direct descendant of my neck, creating an earthworm illusion. I wore a plaid wool skirt suit that cinched my already wasp-thin waist into near nothingness and a pair of "fitness pumps," Lucite platforms with clear plastic straps that were absolutely purchased on an exotic dancer outfitting website. (Naturally, they were my favorite heels.) I donned the wig I had brought, an old ombre blonde whose acrylic tangles hung limply at my temples, its frizzy malaise haloing my general horsiness. As a finishing step, I was asked to apply makeup poorly, and thus your friendly neighborhood drag queen earthworm began applying drugstore makeup to his ghastly visage: royal-blue eyeshadow, burnt-salmon rouge, and fuchsia lipstick. Or maybe it was more like applying makeup to a horse? Whatever it was, it was unnerving. When I look back at the photos, I see the GEICO Neanderthal in drugstore drag.

DEFYING ALL ODDS, *The Tenant* got picked up and was scheduled to premiere in November of 2018. Arthur had decided on a three-person cast: myself as Trelkovsky; ABT principal Cassandra Trenary, with whom I've worked on various side projects, as Simone Choule; and Kibrea Carmichael, a young contemporary dancer/model, as Stella,

Trelkovsky's love interest. The casting process was fairly arduous, with two invite-only auditions. I had never been on the casting side of a show. It was strange to watch the dancers literally bend over backward in an effort to secure the gig, and to peruse their headshots, which were almost all comical. Headshots tend to feature awkward peering over the shoulder, teeth whitened to a smooth baleen appearance, hands and fingers prominently featured caressing the face, and heads cocked at "Do you want a treat?" angles.

Cassandra (Cassie) won the part of Simone easily, with her proficiency in contemporary ballet and natural sense of theatrics. The role of Stella posed more of an issue. After two auditions, we weren't happy with our options. Nina, Arthur's best friend and ballet master, suggested we look at a young dancer she had seen on Instagram.

Kibrea is a young woman with large Disney eyes and a short, flat-topped, Grace Jones–esque do. She wears only catsuits—black leotards with black leggings and black sneakers or black pumps—showing off arms and legs that sprout from a torso so short it appears to be a small tube, like someone affixed long wooden broomsticks to a single Tootsie Roll. It's absolutely stunning. She's very young, delightfully likable, unbelievably jubilant, and enjoys making grand declarations about her life simply to get a response from the old curmudgeons (myself included). Conversations with young people often feel as though everything they say is just to draw out the desired response. Old people disguise their manipulations with much greater mystery. One must approach conversation with Kibrea as though she were a cat, earning her trust and proving oneself worthy of true candidness.

With Kibrea cast as Stella, we began the creation period for *The Tenant*. Arthur clearly had a system. He bought index cards on which he wrote integral plot points and taped them sequentially to the wall. He'd often pull a chair over to the wall of cards, sit down with his glasses perched on the tip of his nose, cross his legs, and bop his be-socked foot to an inaudible beat. We worked daily in NYC for two weeks, stopping only for iced coffee and falafel. As we completed different scenes, Arthur used a neon-pink highlighter to color in a progress bar on each index card. It was exhilarating to see the cards turn pink with the passage of time.

NEXT UP WAS a monthlong residency at the Lake Placid Center for the Arts, and this is where the unimaginable, harrowing trials began. Arthur, Nina, Cassie, Kibrea, Frank (the composer), Colleen (the props manager), Will (the stage manager), and I took an Amtrak train upstate. But when we arrived at the arts center, there was no one there to meet us, and our cell phones had no service at all. The whole situation had an air of "You're all about to be murdered and fed to alligators."

Finally Arthur stumbled upon the offices and returned to us with Jackie Oranges, a jolly-looking mountain homosexual with squinty eyes and straight black hair. He was friendly and introduced himself to everyone.

"The residence is downstairs," he told us, leading us down a long stairwell into the depths of the earth. "The offices used to be down here, but it was too depressing, so we moved the residence downstairs instead."

At the base of the stairs, the first room we encountered was the laundry room, which should have been called the Mold Farm. Linens, sheets, and towels were balled up and discarded in every nook, creating soiled towers of human despair and emitting a scent of teenage jockstrap.

We continued down the dim hallway. The floor of the entire complex was made up of large Cheeto-orange linoleum squares, and as the basement used to be the offices, the lighting was fluorescent. The rooms had already been assigned, and the next room we encountered was slated to be occupied by Cassie and Kibrea. Peeking into their room, we saw hundreds of lamps. "We call this room 'Lamp Room,'" Jackie Oranges said, with a homicidal smirk. A large cabinet in the center of the room acted as a partition between the beds, presumably so its occupants could masturbate in secrecy.

Next were the complex's dormitory-like bathrooms, which housed two standing showers with vinyl shower curtains from 1942. They were so moldy that they seemed to be home to entire microcivilizations. The next room was Frank's. After that was mine, a square that housed three full beds.

The common area was in shambles. It was as if everyone's grandmothers had dumped their furniture into one room. It wasn't incongruous in a chic way; it was pandemonium! Arthur and Cassie were particularly affronted by this room and made it a top priority to feng shui it, reorganizing everything and using the vast stores of the Lamp Room to avoid any use of the office lighting.

The whole residence was besieged by multitudinous flies, but the kitchen got the worst of it. They were everywhere. Every surface was covered in a gooey, sticky residue. It became very clear that we would have to clean the place fastidiously to be comfortable, which was futile, because we were to be underground for a month without any windows. Even the folks on the International Space Station can look out a goddamned window.

We called the residence "the Bunker." We were scheduled to live and work on a psychological horror play for a month in an underground place with no windows. We were going to go mad.

(A side note here on the town of Lake Placid. It turned out that the rest of the town was just as confounding as the arts center. It gives one the impression that it was once very chic, yet now it seems like a budget vacation destination. Nearly everyone we met in town was very rude and could sense that we were outsiders, with the exception of a morbidly obese little boy who looked right in my eyes at a local restaurant, singing Rihanna's "Umbrella" in a precious falsetto. He was awesome. I was instructed to avoid using Grindr during the residency, because apparently homophobes in Lake Placid use it to lure men into their homes to kill them. I'm absolutely certain they fuck them first, though. Tackiness abounded: during one donor event at a local "rich" person's house, all the dancers were made to wear spray-painted, glittery Burger King crowns, supposedly so we could be distinguished from the other guests. The food was truly terrible, too. There was a restaurant next to the Bunker called Desperados that served MexiQuinn food, which they defined as Irish Mexican food. We tried it and can confidently say that this is a thing that should not exist.)

After spending our first night in the Bunker, it was time to get to work. Unfortunately, we were alerted by Jackie Oranges that we would not have a studio to work in for the next three days because of children's dance classes.

"Well then, WHAT THE FUCK ARE WE DOING HERE?!" we asked.

In response, he gave us a detailed schedule that would allow us to work for an hour here, an hour there. The issue was that we had dozens of props and set pieces, and the point of the residency was to make a show in one room for a month. Finally, we managed to work it out so we could remain in one studio while not inconveniencing the four-year-olds of Lake Placid too much.

WE WORKED FOR about a week and a half without incident, eating lovely group dinners and playing rummy while drinking copiously into the night. But one night, during the second week, my throat grew sore and I began to feel feverish. Much like when I had gotten sick during the workshop process, I felt as if I were underwater. Earlier that day, we'd happened to be working on the scene in *The Tenant* in which Trelkovsky gets an intense fever, begins shaking uncontrollably, and drags himself to the doctor. We rehearsed it over and over again. I'd fall to the floor, begin shivering, and rush out to the pretend doctor. My life was becoming Trelkovsky's life.

I went to sleep, hoping I'd wake up feeling better, but awoke around one a.m. and ran to the bathroom. I forcefully vomited everything I had eaten that day, then turned around and forcefully ejected diarrhea directly into my vomit. I was like a supermassive black hole, expelling matter in opposing relativistic jets damn close to the speed of light.

Then the fever came. I began shivering. I would take two-hour naps between trips to the restroom for black-hole matter expulsion. I found myself sitting on the high-pile toilet mat, face inches from the moldy shower curtains. Trelkovsky was very ill indeed.

The next morning I was driven to the local urgent care center. I was barely conscious. An indeterminate amount of minutes, hours, or years later, a doctor shuffled into my small examination room. He was middle-aged and wore gray sweatpants instead of scrubs. On his feet were Skechers sneakers, the ones that are curved on the bottom and marketed as "diet shoes," and he had a bursting-at-the-seams fanny pack on. A doctor . . . with a fanny pack. It was as if Robin Williams's reanimated corpse was about to diagnose me.

He took my temperature, which was nine hundred degrees Fahrenheit, did a rapid strep test (which never seems to work), and checked my vitals. My rapid strep test came back negative, even though I knew I had strep. He prescribed me penicillin and sent me on my way.

The bottle instructed me to eat a full meal before taking the medication, and there was a McDonald's next door, so I tried my luck. I was in good spirits. I was sick, but I held the cure in the palm of my hand. All I needed was a biscuit sandwich and an orange juice and then I'd be right as rain.

After wolfing down my biscuit and taking my pills, I was so optimistic that I decided to venture to celebrate somebody's birthday that evening. I don't even know whose birthday it was. I slept most of the day, but tried to reanimate for the evening's festivities. It was hopeless. I went right back to sleep and woke up like clockwork, vomiting and shaking from fever.

This nasty schedule continued for days, with no sign of improvement. It actually worsened. My appetite diminished to practically nothing, and I found drinking even water repulsive. Arthur and Nina tried to help by giving me "teas" that consisted of boiled garlic, ginger, and apple cider vinegar. I'd sit in my dark room in the Bunker, shivering, sweating, and trying to force yogurt down my gullet. My room smelled like laundry you forgot to put in the dryer, body odor, and farts. When I'd soak one of the beds in my dungeon with sweat, I'd hobble over to one of the others. It was a cycle of sickly, sweaty, wetness. It was time to revisit the doctor.

Instead of going back to fanny-pack Frankenstein, Will took me to the emergency room. I recall being alone for a long time in a cold metal examination room, barely conscious and muttering "I'm so cold" to myself over and over again. The doctor finally entered, made a scrunched-up face, walked over to the window, and opened it. He asked me if I took any medications regularly.

I said, "Yes, I take PrEP. Truvada."

He didn't know what it was. The doctor didn't know what PrEP was. Another red flag. Truvada, aka PrEP, is a daily pill that greatly reduces the risk of contracting HIV.

"So, you have AIDS?" the doctor said.

"No, I'm trying *not* to get HIV," I replied.

He barely understood. He looked at my throat and said, "Looks like herpes." I thought to myself, "He only thinks it's herpes because I'm a gay man who's taking an HIV preventative."

I knew it wasn't herpes, as tests later confirmed, and asked him to look at the penicillin I had been taking. "This is for kids," he said, and laughed. I had been taking medication intended for a forty-five-pound child. "No wonder you're not getting better." I was close to tears. He prescribed me a new, higher dosage of antibiotics and I was on my way.

I remember very little of the next few days in the Bunker. My fever did not subside, and my shivering and vomiting worsened. In between Tylenol naps, I'd read chapters from Roald Dahl's *Boy*, which actually ended up being the inspiration for writing this book.

I began to hallucinate. While lying in my Cheeto-colored lino-leum tomb, I would hear my alarm going off. It was maddening. I could see that my phone was silent, clearly not going off in any way, but I heard my alarm swelling in my mind. I spent days trying to ignore the sound. It was as though my subconscious mind was saying, "Get up! You're supposed to be making a show, goddamn it!"

I spent a lot of time on the toilet, as I suffered from what my mother called "eeyahdeeyah." She didn't like saying the word *diarrhea*. While seated on the porcelain throne, I would stare at the door to the stall, and in its wooden grains, I saw two lovers, locked in a kiss. I visited them often and their positions moved and swayed. They'd release their lips from one another to turn to face me on the toilet, struggling with eeya-deeyah, and say in unison, "Quit shitting and get back to work."

My condition only worsened. Cassie, Nina, and Arthur decided it was best for me to get out of the Bunker. How was a person supposed to get well in a moldy, windowless room? They moved me into a motel across the street called Wildwood on the Lake. I don't know how I got there and I don't know who packed my things. I was in my bed shaking in the Bunker, and then I was in my bed shaking at Wildwood.

I woke up from a hallucinatory alarm-clock nap and went down-stairs to the reception desk, which was staffed by a girl who appeared

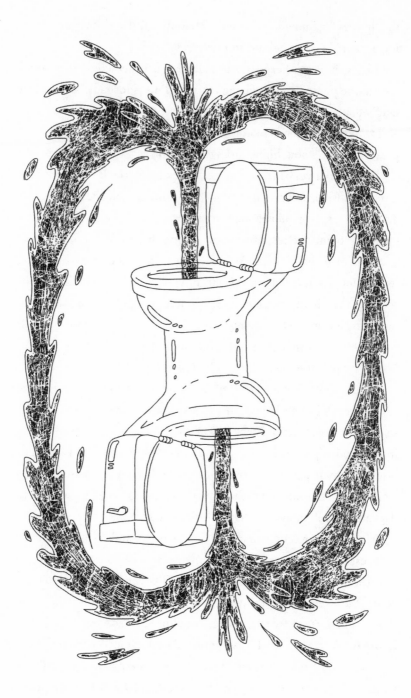

to be in her late teens and who was wearing the native costume of the region: jeans and flannels.

"What's the Wi-Fi?" I asked her quietly.

She looked at me long and strange and replied, "It's how you get on the internet."

I stared back at her. "No," I said slowly, "I know that. What's the network and password?"

"Ummmm, oh, I get it. It's right here on this card."

"Thanks."

"Ummmm, like how long do you think you're gonna be here?"

"In this hotel? I'm not sure. Why? Do you need the room by a certain date?"

"Ummmm, no."

"Then what does it matter?"

"What?"

"Why do you need to know when I'm checking out if no one else needs the room?"

"Well . . . I'm not sure."

I skulked back up to my room. My beloved room! With windows! I nearly cried. After weeks of being very, very ill in a dark, musty, windowless room, I had made it topside and was greeted by a room with windows and cable television. My mood swung up in a wonderful way and I thought to myself, "I'm going to get better now."

I inspected the motel further. Everything looked to have been built in the 1970s. There was burnt-sienna wall-to-wall carpeting, plaid burnt-sienna curtains, and plaid burnt-sienna bed linens. The television was obviously found at a tag sale in 1987. I turned it on and there was a marathon of *American Dad!*, which I adore. I was on the second floor, and the windows opened onto an unofficial terrace, which was just the flat roof of the first floor. I peeked out and there was an upstate hillbilly sitting on a woven fabric lawn chair. He was wearing what looked like a redneck costume: a trucker hat, a plaid button-down shirt with the sleeves cut off, boot-cut jeans, and flip-flops. In his right hand was a Coors Light and in his left, a cigarette. He looked directly at me and we locked eyes. By this point I resembled some sort of convalescent Skeletor (from *He-Man*), and I could see his mind working out a question: "Is that one of those queers come here to die?"

Even with the window, my illness worsened. My fever continued and I was unable to eat anything. I was literally wasting away. I could see the hillbilly creepily sitting outside my window, peering in every now and again. The weird girl at the front desk called me every day to ask, "Ummm . . . are you leaving today?" Cassie texted me to ask if she could bring me anything. I didn't want anyone to see me like this, so I said no. Thankfully she ignored me and knocked on my door that evening. She had brought a pizza and was determined to make me eat something. I sat bundled on my bed, looking like a little sea cucumber, and tried to eat a bit of the pizza. I found it nauseating and slipped back into my feverish shakes. Cassie was really rattled by my condition, which had worsened over the last few days. She kept bringing me cold, wet towels to put on my forehead. I fell asleep and she vowed to return in the morning.

The following morning she showed up with a blueberry muffin and said, "You have to eat." She fed me a bit of the muffin, which I chewed in my dry mouth for what felt like a month before saying, "I can't." "Oh, yes you can," she said and guided a straw into my mouth. "It's water," she said. I macerated a bit of the blueberry muffin into a muffin smoothie and barely got it down before my shakes began again. I began to sob, "What is happening to me? It's been weeks."

Alarmed, Cassie called Arthur and said, "I don't think James can stay here."

When I awoke from another hallucinatory fever sleep, Cassie was still there. She said, "You're going back to the city." I said, "OK. I can take the train. I'll be fine." I spent the rest of that morning in and out of consciousness, with Cassie efficiently packing my things into my suitcase to the sound of *American Dad!* playing quietly on the eighties television. I awoke only to vomit or shake uncontrollably. I heard Cassie call Arthur again. "There's no way he can be alone on a train." After she hung up, she sat down next to me and said, "Will is going to drive you back to the city."

I said feebly, "No. I can't make him do that."

"Well, that's what's going to happen. I'll wake you up when it's time to go," she whispered.

I was awakened by Cassie, Arthur, and Will. They dressed me and helped me down the stairs to where Will's SUV was waiting, with the rest of the cast and crew. They had removed the seats and packed the prop mattress into the back, creating a makeshift ambulance. There were pillows and blankets and everything. I had my hood pulled tight over my head and was wearing dark dad sunglasses because the light made my head throb. As I scooted back onto the pillows, I began to weep. "I'm so sorry," I said. "I can't believe how kind you all are. I can't believe you did this." I was moved by their tenderness and am still so grateful for their care.

After the six-hour drive, during which I was barely conscious, Will and I dropped my bags off at my apartment. I was fully reenacting the "Thriller" music video by this point. My desiccated corpse was being led by my sheer will to live. I hailed a taxi, which took me to my doctor's office. "Dr. O," I call him. I feel that he's the first doctor I've had since childhood who actually cares about my survival. His knowledge is extensive and his network vast, and he's had his own practice in the East Village since the big bang. This gentle, kind man has had the unpleasant misfortune to be my primary care physician.

I am a fragile little queen. I get strep throat all the time, as I'm too lazy and stubborn to get my tonsils out. "But how will I rehearse?!" I ask incredulously whenever anyone suggests it. As a result, Dr. O knows me well, so when I walked into his office looking like a goddamned feather in the wind, he nearly had a heart attack.

"Wh-wha-wh-what ha-ha-happened?" he asked. I forgot to mention that Dr. O has an adorable and very charming stutter, like a genius toddler.

I informed him that I had been mistreated. "I've been locked in a basement where the internet was bad!" I started crying, wincing each time a magma tear oozed over my knifelike cheekbones.

He took my temperature, which was approximately 105 degrees, no hyperbole. He then took me by the arm and shoulder and walked me the two short Manhattan blocks to Mount Sinai Beth Israel hospital. I remember how bright the sun was and how I knew it was bizarre that such bright sunlight should make me shiver. Extreme sickness makes common occurrences seem brutal and alien.

When we entered the hospital, I was put in a wheelchair, and Dr. O demanded that I be helped immediately. He told the doctors on the floor that I had a blood infection from a persistent throat infection that had been treated incorrectly. His tone was so sure. I was grateful to finally have an idea of what the hell was wrong with me. I was put in a room and immediately put on intravenous antibiotics. Dr. O went back to his practice and said he'd return after the workday.

The hospital doctors crowded around me. They each, in turn, shone a bright flashlight in each of my pupils, noting how I shuddered and blanched. They looked like hand-drawn charcoal monsters, twitching and writhing above me. I'd see flashes of their hideously distorted physiques between flashlight assaults. They aahed and hmmed each time I shrank away from the light. Sinking down over me, their faces pressed together like the petals of a hellflower, they said in multitonal, demonic unison, "We'll need to do a spinal tap. We think you have meningitis, and in that case you'll be dead in a week, if not a few days."

Half-conscious, I managed to croak out, "No. Please, no. Dr. O. He's right. I know it. Wait until the IV starts working. What's a few hours if I'll be dead in a week?"

The wraiths obliged the shriveled husk under their piglike snouts and dispersed.

I laid there, wondering if it was true. I saw and heard things, still a victim to fevered hallucinations. I imagined needles snapping in my veins and piercing through my skin. I heard screams from other hospital beds, unintelligible gibberish.

Only one thing outweighed my fear of death, and that was my reluctance to tell my loved ones that I was dying. Even on the precipice, I wanted to protect my facade of strength. During my time in the hospital, I never once called or texted my father. I didn't want to scare him, which is unbelievably selfish of me. I didn't tell anyone—not even my boyfriend, who was doing a drag show in India, of all places— except my friend Jeff, who visited daily and brought me clean clothes and delicious orange Gatorade. I didn't post about my illness on social media, even though I know many people who jizz at the thought of garnering internet sympathy.

Dr. O was correct: my blood had become infected because of the lack of correct treatment for my throat infection. I'm grateful to the hospital demons for heeding my decrees to leave my spine untapped. On the fourth day of my hospital stay, after much sleep and convalescent hours gratefully watching Peg Bundy mince about in syndicated reruns of *Married . . . with Children*, I was ejected back into the bright Manhattan sunlight.

I stepped out onto the East Village sidewalk weak and grateful. I even chose to forgo popping in my headphones and listening to music on my walk home. I wanted to hear the sounds of the city that I was robbed of during my time as an inmate at the Lake Placid Dungeon. New York City seemed more vibrant than ever. The taxis streaked by a vibrant mac-and-cheese yellow, and the sky vibrated azure like a

1980s neon nail salon. All the passersby had ravines of worry marking their preoccupied faces, and walked at a pace that would equal a suburban sprint.

I thought of my mother, who spent close to a year dying, and ascertained that I'd like to spend as little time dying as possible. I thought about how much more life I wanted to achieve, the first goal being the completion and performance of *The Tenant*, which I had worked so hard for, only to be derailed by illness. I would NOT suffer the same fate that befell my character, Trelkovsky.

I thought of my morbid sentiments from just days before, when I was sure I'd perish in a week due to meningitis. I thought of my choice to keep my illness a secret. If a television or film character had done that, I would have shouted at them. "I did it to protect you," they'd say. Fuck that nonsense. I did it to protect myself. How would I tell someone I was dying? My fear and shame outweighed my desire to include another in my demise.

The mad thing is, I'm still glad I didn't tell anyone. The whole ordeal was made easier by not having a slew of gays weeping over my wizened visage, and that's assuming anyone would come to visit. I often fancy myself a homosexual pariah.

Upon my miraculous recovery, I thought of my guardian angels: the cast and crew of *The Tenant*, Dr. O, my friend Jeff, and the hospital demons. But most of all, I thought of Peg Bundy, whose voice whistled in my brain as I gleefully walked uptown on Second Avenue: "Al Bundy, this is all your fault. I should be up in heaven having sex with a young Elvis."

WHY NOT?

Twink /'twiNGk/

noun

1. TRADEMARK

   a small finger-shaped sponge cake with a white synthetic
   cream filling

2. INFORMAL · OFFENSIVE

   a gay or effeminate man, or a young man regarded as an
   object of homosexual desire

In June of 2009, my friends Prince, Chip, Teena, and I were a rambunctious gaggle of twinks in our early twenties with a mantra: "Why not?" We decided to take the cheapest flight possible to Portland, Oregon, to visit our friend Tony in his new digs. Tony—aka Teena, after his drag name, Nicoteena Patch—had recently moved to

Portland to dance for Oregon Ballet Theatre, after Boston Ballet fired him and many of our other friends during 2008's economic crisis. I had never been to the West Coast and was immediately struck by the stark contrast to East Coast American behavior. Everyone dressed as though they shopped at either a mall or an outdoor sports store. There were long-haired hippies in flip-flops, women with suntanned skin and bare midriffs, and dreadlocks in abundance. As I emerged from the plane into the Oregon summer sunlight, I happily let the parody of West Coast living play out before me.

When Teena's then-boyfriend, Alexander, asked us to go to the outdoor marketplace, we employed our mantra, jovially replying, "Why not?" Alexander wouldn't let us call him Alex. He was thin and bow-legged, wore gauzy rags, and had a rattail. We immediately hated him. He'd preach West Coast comedy at us like, "NO. Listen to me. Are you *be*? Do you ever just *be*?" I still don't know what that was supposed to mean. We'd roll our cynical northeastern eyes and ask to turn up the music inside Teena's boxy car, which we'd nicknamed "Toastine" because it looked like a toaster. We smoked a joint in the car as we pulled up to the marketplace blasting Lady Gaga's "Boys Boys Boys."

Stepping out of the car wearing our H&M finery, we were assaulted by a loud, gleeful din, colors and shapes of all sizes, and a multicultural bombardment of scents. Each street corner blasted a different song by Michael Jackson, who had just died. His death had gravitas. Just as I will forever remember where I was when Princess Diana died, the same goes for Michael Jackson. His *HIStory* was one of the first CDs I ever owned and made dances to in the privacy of my childhood bedroom. As we continue to inspect his life postmortem, to autopsy his choices and ambiguities, I feel a heaviness in my chest and a lump in my throat. When I listen to songs like "Man in the Mirror" or "Human Nature," I smile-cry through them. I am incredulous and also incredibly aware of the magic. He and his music are beauty and terror and everything that it is to exist.

Toddlers, teens, adults, and the elderly danced in the streets, drinking out of red Solo cups filled with various tipples. The sun shone down as a fresh breeze ruffled the tulle skirts of the reveling gender rebels. Teena and I joined a dance circle and performed our best moves for a large crowd as "Beat It" screamed from a boom box. It was pure joy, a happiness that only friendship, sunshine, and good music can elicit.

The following day, we took Toastine up the coast to see the sights in Seattle. We were bopping around from tourist attraction to tourist attraction when some Washington-based dancers, Dylan and Chad, invited us to dinner and a Pride party. Dylan and Chad were married homosexuals. They were both incredibly attractive, as their names suggest. I had heard that they had an open relationship, which meant they could have sex with people other than their spouse. They were the first open couple I had ever (knowingly) met. I was fascinated and flirted with them shamelessly over dinner at the restaurant.

Dinner concluded and we made our way to the party. We drove Toastine there with the intention of going back to Portland that night, as we didn't have a place to crash in Seattle or the funds to purchase a hotel room. The party was truly epic, as only parties in your early twenties can be. My flirtatiousness was working and it was clear to me that Dylan and Chad were interested in sleeping with me. As the party wore on and the drunkenness crescendoed, they asked me to leave with them.

I had just celebrated my one-year anniversary with Dan and we were in a monogamous relationship at the time. I warred with myself on what to do. My gift for denial kicked in and I obliged them, saying, "OK. But we can't *do* anything." Complete and utter nonsense. I found my friends to tell them. They were all sniffing after their own vittles. I bid them goodnight and told them I'd call them soon.

Dylan and Chad's apartment seemed like the most luxe, posh place I'd ever seen. Chad was a well-known dancer and therefore I assumed him to be loaded. They made me a drink and brought me up to their bedroom, where they tried to kiss me.

"I can't," I said futilely. "I'm in a relationship."

Nevertheless, they both got completely naked, and my eyes were assaulted by two of the largest, most overwhelming penises I had ever experienced. I removed my clothes and wedged myself between them in the bed. I was such a freak. I wouldn't let them perform oral sex on me and I lay there guiltily as they greedily ran their hands all over my body. What I had intended to be a staunchly defiant rebuttal of advances turned into an incredibly sexy affair. It was an amazing game of cat and mouse in which they pushed me to submit to their exhilarating ministrations. We essentially just had an edgy wank together, then played *Wii Tennis* before I guiltily took a taxi back to meet my friends.

I felt very affected by the night's occurrences and was torn as to whether I should tell Dan about it. In retrospect, the whole scene was rather innocuous, considering how our lives have shifted since then, from monogamous to open to separated. But at the time, I was shaken, hungover, and exhausted. I didn't end up telling Dan about it until eleven years later. He just laughed and said, "Work."

EARLY THE NEXT MORNING, I met up with my friends at a Stumptown Coffee shop to hear about their respective debaucheries. The morning-after summary was something I always looked forward to within our friend group. We always met at a diner or a coffee shop after a night out to exchange stories and tales of licentiousness. Prince had ended up meeting a handsome Cuban gentleman and hooking up with him in the back of his car. He nicknamed him "Cuban Sausage" and says that to this day, he had the biggest penis he'd ever seen. Teena and Chip had had a threesome during which Teena left, effectively passing off the dick as though it were a baton in a relay race.

We groggily drove Toastine back down the coast to Portland and passed out at Teena's until the next morning, when we decided it was time for a trip to the gay nude beach. We pulled up blasting Gaga's "Summerboy" out of Toastine's rolled-down windows. Music has the power to incite and instigate certain behaviors, which I like very much. "Bikini tops, coming oh, oh, off!" Gaga mewled, and Teena had barely exited the car when he pulled off his Speedo.

We set up our towels on a rocky stretch by the water. Old men gazed lasciviously at the twinks spreading out performatively on their Disney towels. Bears jostled each other, spilling their Budweisers and flirtatiously tweaking each other's nipples. Lesbians spread tanning oil on their lovers and friends. Music wafted on the breeze, blowing in from various devices and boats on the water. The sun danced a jig with feathery clouds, making the blue sky seem impossibly deep.

Teena saw a beautiful boat on the water and said, "Let's swim out to that boat." There was a gentleman standing at the wheel and drinking a beer. "He looks kinda cute," Teena said. We stood up, completely nude, and sauntered down to the edge of the water. Our feet lazily lapped by the waves and our dicks to the wind, we waved frantically to the man in the boat. He perked up and waved us out. Smirking at each other, we ran into the water like adorable naked little kids, our penises thrashing to and fro.

We arrived at the boat's ladder out of breath and cold from the early summer water. Our rescuer handed us each a plush, fluffy towel, which we wrapped cozily around our skinny frames, and offered us beers. He introduced himself as Steve as he took long pulls from a Marlboro Red and sipped a Pabst Blue Ribbon. He was of medium height and build, with a sunburned nose and the tan lines and eye wrinkles of a farmer. His impossibly blue eyes were beautiful but also betrayed hints of crazy. As I always say, "The crazy lies within the eyes." His nails were dirty and he looked as rough as they come. He wore long navy-blue board shorts with no shirt, showing off a slight paunch and a bare chest that had a small patch of hair at the center. Steve appeared to be in his early forties, which to a twenty-one-year old looked ancient. He vaguely resembled the quarterback Tom Brady, if Tom Brady were a potato farmer and a lush.

Prince, Chip, and I took turns taking photos of each other in splits and high kicks. Teena was up at the captain's seat getting a driving lesson from Steve. From where we were sitting at the bow, we could vaguely see Teena flirting with Steve. Then we saw Steve kneel in front of Teena to perform oral sex, a Marlboro Red still clutched in his left hand as his right reached around to grab an ass cheek. Teena seemed to be enjoying himself until he suddenly yelped, "Ow! My dick! YOU BURNED MY DICK!" He skittered down to the bow of the boat and told us, "Shit. He burned my dick."

The sun was setting and Uncle Steve, as we'd started calling our boat daddy, asked if we'd want to go to his beach house the following day. "It's quite a drive and you'd have to pick up the keys from my forest home first," he warned us. But when presented with an invitation, it was our civic duty to reply, "Why not?" We gave him our information, thanked him for a fun day, and headed back to shore.

Inside Toastine, we wondered what exactly we were getting ourselves into. Why not? Why not? *Why not?* Apprehension thus effectively ignored, we continued on our merry way, laughing at our fortune and screaming along to "Money Honey."

The following morning, as we piled our weekend bags and our cute twink butts into Toastine for a little beach house retreat to Uncle Steve's, we began to realize how strange what we were doing was. We didn't know this guy. He could be a murderer, for all we knew. It would be like any horror film. The unwitting, imbecile twinks mince directly into the patiently waiting open maw of a monster while the viewer shouts, "WHAT THE FUCK! NO! GET OUT OF THERE!"

"Shit. We're gonna get killed, but I hope I get fucked first!" Teena said.

We printed out directions from MapQuest, a hilarious site from the pre-GPS era. I remember shuffling the pages about, trying to discern which went where. We wove in and out of trees, traversing lush glens and marveling at the sun-dappled splendor of Oregon's natural beauty. I had never seen such exquisite forests. I felt as though I had entered a beloved Hayao Miyazaki film and was to be greeted by wood nymphs and water sprites. But instead we were driving toward Uncle Steve, the dick burner from Portland.

Finally we arrived at the dirt-road driveway for Uncle Steve's forest home. At the end of the drive stood a majestic wooden structure with beautiful windows. The house looked like a hybrid of a 1950s cathedral and a Fire Island Pines masterpiece. It was completely wooden, and enormous oak trees swayed alongside it. There were various metal sculptures on the grounds and rolling, green-canopied hills. We were gobsmacked by the beauty. Teena whispered in awe, "Shit. Let's get *murdered*."

Uncle Steve gleefully burst from the front door and shouted, "Welcome!"

Prince said, "Is that a butthole?" There was an enormous iron sculpture flanking the flagstones leading toward the front door. It stood nine feet tall on a pole and was approximately nine square feet of folded and worked iron, with all its folds originating from a central anus.

"Yes, that's our famous anus sculpture."

"Oh my fucking god, it's a big butthole!" Teena screamed in delight, and cackled as Chip posed for a photo with it as if he were posing with Michelle Obama, with whom he is obsessed. His pride was *that* visible. Chip has a way of smiling like he's never been so happy as at that exact moment, but then he smiles the same way a bit later and you wonder if he's ever *not* happy. Chip's laughter is like the laughter of a toddler. It's impossible to suppress a smile. The way he smiled next to that monolithic poop chute outweighs the *Mona Lisa*, in my mind.

Uncle Steve brought us into the house and introduced us to his friend, who was so dry and bland he could best be described as hay. The house looked as though it was under construction and had the distinct aura of a homosexual crack house. I am almost certain it was a place of either drug production or porn production. Nevertheless, we were amazed by its sheer size. Rich people were still like unicorns to me at that point in my life. I have since realized that 99 percent of the 1 percent are insufferable.

We were led through the house and greeted in each of the many rooms by homoerotic art—sculptures, paintings, drawings, and artifacts of myriad shapes and sizes, each depicting strange and beautiful gay scenes. I had met only a few older gay people by this point in my life, but it seemed that all their homes represented how thankful they were to be homosexual. Each room shone with a pride that bludgeoned you. At the time, I found it a touch overwrought, but as I age, it makes more and more sense. When enough people tell you that you shouldn't exist, it makes you want to scream, "FUCK YOU, I EXIST!" And the older the gay man, the more volcanic his fury.

Uncle Steve and the man made out of hay wanted to show us the pride of their home, The Observatory, so we walked up a floating wooden staircase to a small room shaped like a turret. It was completely windowed, creating a dome of glass with a beautiful view of the robin's-egg sky resting lazily on a bushy green canopy. The glamour of looking up was not mirrored by looking down, however. On the floor lay a bare full mattress, a box fan, an old tube television, and a stack of gay porn DVDs.

I don't know what they expected us to do, but we sure didn't do it. Instead, Teena said, "It's a dick observatory! Prince, take my picture." Prince always carried a small digital camera with him—it was before the time of smartphone cameras—and he obliged as Teena jumped on the crack den observatory mattress, posing in his too-big sunglasses and his fauxhawk hairstyle.

Uncle Steve and Hay then sent us out to play in the backyard, which was a sprawling field resplendent with wildflowers. Like young Alices, we lay down in the flowers and wished we could talk to them for hours. As we were fondled by a gentle breeze, a pale waxing-gibbous moon looked down on us and whispered, "*Bottoms.*"

Upon our return to the house, Uncle Steve asked if we wanted to see his cock. Then, with a lascivious wink, he said, "My chicken," and presented us with his pet chicken, Marissa. I silently barfed into my hands and then ate it back up to rid myself of the evidence.

The sun was skirting the horizon as we were handed the keys to the beach house and given directions. We thanked Uncle Steve and Hay profusely for their generosity and then got into Toastine and began our long trek to the coast of Oregon.

When we finally arrived at the beach house, bouncing along rocky beach roads to "Beautiful, Dirty, Rich," the light had been completely replaced by extreme, black night. Oregon's nature continued to astound me. We unloaded our things from Toastine and entered the house, which was on a small jetty and seemed to be suspended over the ocean itself—a wooden island in a raging, spiteful sea. Turning on a light, we were once again gobsmacked by our twinkly good fortune. The floor was covered by a lush 1960s carpet, and the floor-to-ceiling windows were framed by wood-paneled walls and large, heavy beams. There were happy houseplants and large, overstuffed settees. The beach house was not ostentatious in its richness. It was concise, cozy, and perched atop the misty waves.

After exploring the house and selecting our rooms, we took blankets outside and spread out under the stars. Zero light pollution affected this remote corner of the earth. We laughed and marveled at the visible swirl of the galaxy above us, and talked about existentialism and metaphysics like twenty-somethings. Freezing and exceedingly grateful to have not yet been murdered, we went back inside and headed to bed.

The following morning, Teena came into the living room and said, "Shit. Uncle Steve texted me. He said he's coming up to the beach house." Now we were *sure* our disembowelment was imminent. We thought we were going to have the place to ourselves, and having Uncle Steve there would surely change the dynamic. He arrived shortly thereafter and the whole place took on a sinister mien. Each dark corner of the house became a black hole. The waves smashing against the rocks became a death march. Uncle Steve drank copiously and followed us around the house. We were waiting for the moment when he'd snap and gut us for pie ingredients.

Luckily, we had a distraction. A few days earlier, at the nude beach, Teena had run into a benefactor of the arts. His name was Jean and he was a very handsome older gentleman. This man was *definitely* someone I'd be happy to meet now. He had invited us to join him at his vineyard the upcoming weekend, and we obliged. The next day, we would bounce from one outrageous situation to the next.

The other twinks and I had recently learned about the Radical Faeries, a countercultural movement seeking to evaporate the commercialization of queer culture. To thank Jean for his generosity, we decided that our visit to the vineyard should climax in a performance as Radical Faeries. We mixed various songs together and choreographed an elaborate dance in the 1960s kitchen of Uncle Steve's beach house while he watched, a martini in hand and a cigarette dangling from his sunburned lips. We thought if we ignored him, he might go away. What we didn't think about was that he was probably just making sure the idiot twinks he had invited to his beautiful home didn't burn the joint down. When we went to our rooms that night, we locked our doors for fear of Uncle Steve's murderous advances . . . which we had invented. We set our alarms for the crack of dawn, because we were convinced that if we stayed any longer, we'd end up outlined in chalk.

The next morning, all of us twinks bid a grateful and wary farewell to Uncle Steve, who stood perplexed and half-asleep in the doorway of the stunning beach house that we'd never see again, and loaded ourselves into Toastine. We zipped down the coast toward Jean's vineyard, shouting our lyrical take on Lady Gaga's "LoveGame":

I wanna fist you
But if I do, then I might get poo hands

JEAN WAS THE VERSION OF Uncle Steve that didn't enjoy booze or meth. His money was very shiny gay money instead of mattress money. He greeted us in a crisp white button-down, short-sleeved shirt, a pair of Jesus-like sandals, and pressed khaki shorts that showed off the fine hair of his legs. His hair was carefully coiffed and fluffing about in the July breeze. If Uncle Steve was a bucking bronco, Jean was a My Little Pony. He wasn't very effeminate, but he was just so *clean*. His straight, whiter-than-white teeth flashed in the summer sun as he welcomed us to his vast and sprawling vineyard, which was full of infinite rows of grapevines. Its organized composition was also a stark contrast to Uncle Steve's butthole forest home and 1960s beach house.

We had spent the long drive constructing makeshift Radical Faeries costumes from materials we had bought at JOANN, and had changed into them in the car so we could make a grand entrance. Jean took us to a small hospitality house, where polite and quiet staff in cream-colored uniforms served us—extreme homosexuals wearing itty-bitty panties, tulle, glitter, and feathers—glass after glass of fine wine on adorable platters. I can't help but feel that Jean wasted his wine on us, as we weren't terribly discerning oenophiles.

Toasted by the sun and buzzed from a wine tasting, we decided it was time for our thank you performance as Radical Faeries. Jean gathered his friends and staff and sat on a hill adjacent to the long rows of vines. Our glittering costumes twinkled in the afternoon sun as we set up our portable speaker and pressed play. The dance was absurdly hilarious, but also sexual without actually being sexy. We grabbed each other's asses, performed mock fellatio, and shook our butts to an ever-changing cheerleader megamix containing everything from Beyoncé to Tchaikovsky. Our petite audience laughed and applauded effusively when we finished. Teena was wearing a dog toy as a codpiece, so we all took turns slapping it to make a loud squeaking noise.

As the sun began to set, we stretched out on the highest hill of the vineyard, framed by little yellow buttercups and feeling the immense joy of being ourselves. There was a distinct magic in the air. Velvety lilac clouds wafted past us as we regaled each other with tales from just an hour ago, giggling and congratulating ourselves.

OUR MANTRA HAD fully paid off in outrageous ways, so when we returned to Portland and one of Teena's coworkers, Gennaro, invited us to a gay club on our final night, we felt obliged to reply, "Why not?" We showered and primped, styling our hair into spiky, straightened mohawks and donning our most skintight jeans and tank tops.

Gennaro met us at the club with his new boyfriend, who looked just like Jake Gyllenhaal. Gennaro was a short, handsome guy with hair that could have belonged to a Shiba Inu. He had large, brown eyes, a small, straight nose, and lips with a finely arched cupid's bow. His body was tight and right, alluding to his many hours of work in the ballet studio. His boyfriend, whom we referred to as Jake Gyllenhaal because we never bothered to learn his name, was exceptionally tall, with thick-rimmed glasses and a long, chiseled face. His dark, gelled hair was close-cropped and parted at the side. He was hot, nerdy, and socially inept.

Teena, Prince, Chip, and I took turns flirting with Jake Gyllenhaal right in front of Gennaro's unwitting eyes. The night wore on and the vodka sodas kept multiplying. We danced and scream-sang along to the dance pop emanating from the club's plethora of speakers. Queen's "We Are the Champions" blared, and we hoisted Teena up on our shoulders. He grabbed onto the club's decorative chandelier and began swinging from it as onlookers laughed and the song morphed into a mash-up with Gaga's "Speechless." The joy in the room was tangible. It was a magical day topped off with an ecstatic night.

Finally, we found ourselves downing our last-call beverages as the lights came on. "Let's get Taco Bell!" Teena said. We found a taxi outside the club and got in. Somehow, we persuaded Jake Gyllenhaal to come with us, even though Gennaro was nowhere to be found. I imagine he grew tired of our shameless flirting and left in a huff.

In the car, Prince sat on Jake Gyllenhaal's lap, and they started making out at impossible angles. The rest of us laughed and turned up the radio. We begged the cabbie to take us through the Taco Bell drive-through, promising to tip him well. He obliged, and we were on our merry way, six tacos and Crunchwrap Supremes richer.

Arriving at Teena's building, we spilled out of the taxi and made our way up to his studio apartment, where the four of us were staying. Jake Gyllenhaal came up with us, and he and Prince continued their drunken shenanigans. They were both completely inebriated and it was a very comical affair. Teena, Chip, and I peered at them from the kitchen alcove, Crunchwrap Supremes in hand like popcorn at a movie, and giggled at the two of them while trying to remain fairly quiet.

Prince was still trying to discern the general location of Jake Gyllenhaal's anus when suddenly he stood up and ran into the bathroom, where he vomited violently into the toilet. He kept barfing for a long time and did not emerge. Jake Gyllenhaal was still sitting on the bed, masturbating furiously and ignoring the commotion around him. He looked up at Teena and asked, "Got a dildo?"

"Sure!" Teena said and rummaged in a drawer to produce an enormous, double-sided matte black dildo, which he handed to Jake Gyllenhaal. It's a fact: Jake Gyllenhaal loves dildos.

Teena returned to the kitchen alcove and we resumed our places as absurd voyeurs, squirting Fire sauce on our tacos as Jake Gyllenhaal squirted lubricant on a massive, double-headed dildo.

Jake Gyllenhaal's next move would burn itself into my brain for all eternity. When the universe collapses, the following image will still be etched into my mind. Jake Gyllenhaal knelt on the bed, his back to us, and generously lubed up one of the hydra dildo's heads. He then proceeded to wrench his body around and clamp down on one side of the dildo with astoundingly dexterous, primate-like feet. The big black dildo waved in the air like an air puppet at a used-car lot. Holding one side of the dildo with his feet, he guided the other side into the expectant maw of his anus. He proceeded to effectively fuck himself using his feet while he masturbated to completion. We were crying, laughing into our tacos at the absurdity of the scene, while Prince continued to vomit from the bathroom. Jake Gyllenhaal then got dressed and left without saying a word to any of us.

We awoke the next morning with the kind of booze headaches that limit one's ability to see. On our way to the airport, we retold the tales of the week with immediate and giddy nostalgia.

WHEN I THINK OF FRIENDSHIP, I think of this trip: the Michael Jackson street party, hiking in a *Twilight* wood, Cuban Sausage, Dylan and Chad, the nude beach, Uncle Steve, Jean and the vineyard, swinging from the chandelier, and Jake Gyllenhaal's double-sided dildo. I

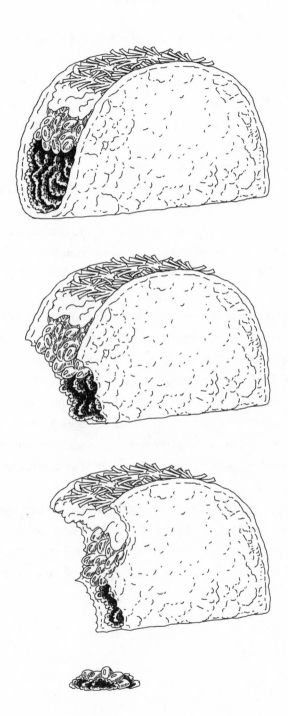

believe we accidentally embodied the mores that the Radical Faeries stand for with all the unintentional success of youth. We were creative, curious, and completely unaware of the pressures of the gay patriarchy. We did no drugs, went to no circuit parties, and planned virtually nothing. Our very existence was bolstered by camp. My friends and I reveled in the newfound ecstasy of our chosen family with all the vigor and courage of the not-yet-jaded. Our actions were founded in the appreciation of each other and of new experiences. We were selfish, but never malicious.

I recall this time wistfully, as I have found that time has complicated life. It's not that life has become more complicated; it's that with age and wisdom comes vision that bares the world before you in all its monstrous glory. I miss *that* type of friendship. The type that allows you to behave with a completely shared reckless abandon. None of the *What can we do for each other?* types of friendships adult lives are riddled with.

I happily remember the Queen lyrics urging us to keep fighting till the end. But then I recall the end has already come—the end of wild youth. Any wildness now is just bad choices. So reader, as you're swinging on the chandelier, "We Are the Champions" will eventually morph into "Speechless," and all your bubble dreams will remain bubble dreams.

But stick around, because eventually, life finds a way to metamorphose into a *new* kind of odyssey. One of knowledge and perseverance. Reckless blindness feels great for a while, freeing you from vicious reality, but soon you'll long for nothing more than the power to *see*.

ACKNOWLEDGMENTS

I'd like to thank my mother for instilling in me a sense of freedom and curiosity, and a general indifference to normalcy. I love you and I miss you every day.

Thank you, Pop, for teaching me to love reading. I am forever grateful to you for always letting me find my own path, while gently guiding me in the generally correct directions. I love you.

Thank you to my siblings, Pete, Missy, Robbie, and Andrew. Our hours-long, midpandemic family Zoom meetings will always be a cherished memory. Discussing Nancy over cigarettes and bottles of Labatt while laughing hysterically should be a requisite family bonding exercise.

Thank you, Cindy, aka Isabella Boylston, and Dan Shin, aka Dshin, for listening to me prattle on about this book for nearly two years. Your sensitivity and advice have shaped my direction and I'm very thankful. I also just like hanging out with you both. You know you're my favorites.

ACKNOWLEDGMENTS

Thank you, Dan Donigan, for supporting all my creative endeavors. Your belief in me has enabled my delusions of grandeur, which I will be forever grateful for.

Thank you, Coop, for being the best friend anyone could ask for. You're an actual angel.

Thank you, Teddy O'Connor, for bringing exactly what I knew you would to this book. Your illustrations are a window into my heart. Your talent and style are perfection. It has been a dream working with you on this and hopefully it's the first of many projects together.

Gretchen Schmid, my tireless editor, thank you from the bottom of my heart for plucking me from the hall of aspiring writers. I truly know that this book would not exist without you. You have given me purpose during a tough time. I finished this book during the COVID-19 pandemic of 2020, when my job as a ballet dancer all but ceased to exist in its natural form, when I split with my boyfriend of twelve years, and when my cat, Ms. Bit, perished after nearly nineteen years. This book, however personal and strange, was paramount to retaining my sanity. I'd also like to thank the marvelous team at Viking for their support of *Center Center*.

Thank you, Cindy Uh, my brilliant literary agent. I bet you didn't know what you were signing on for when I brought you some writing samples! You have done nothing but fight for me and I absolutely wouldn't have come anywhere near publishing a book without you. And Abby Walters, my fabulous cheerleader! Thank you both for taking the time and care to see this book come into the light.

Thank you, Nate Pinsley, for offering me a frigid home in which to write my book. Rhinecliff, your little hamlet, however frozen, was the perfect place to dive into my laptop. Life is a slice of watermelon!

Thank you, Daniel Clark, for your bombastic cover art. I'm so happy to have come across your work on Instagram and can't believe we went from book proposal to published together!

Thank you, Kimberly Giannelli, for your friendship and always being on call for me. I've loved every moment of this journey we've embarked on.

Thank you, Gilda Squire, for joining me as I bring this book to fruition and helping me shine the brightest light on it imaginable. You are absolutely brilliant.

Thank you, Uncle Grant and Aunt Marie. Squam served as the perfect writer's sojourn as I put the finishing touches on this book. I truly appreciate the way you've shared the splendor of that place with me and I will be forever grateful. I look forward to connecting more, post-pandemic!

Jim Luigs, you were actually the first person to read my book in its entirety. Frankly, I'm obsessed with you and I am so glad we met on a beach volleyball court on Fire Island. I value your friendship and respect your work. But most important, I can't wait to get back on the court! "I'm running, I'm running."

And finally, I'd like to thank the countless artists who have shaped the way I think about humor and the world: Roald Dahl, Lewis Carroll, John Tenniel, Seth MacFarlane, David Sedaris, Matt Groening, Tina Fey, Tex Avery, Chuck Jones, and so many more.